DIGITAL GOLD 100 DIGITAL BUSINESS IDEAS

How to start your own online business

Labinot Gashi

ISBN: 9783759723338

Thank you.

I would not be who I am today without the people who have helped me along the way. Every help, big or small, every inspiring conversation has contributed to what this book is today.

First and foremost are my parents, who support us every day wherever they can. Their unceasing commitment and unconditional love form the foundation of my endeavors. To my brother, who is not only a family member but also a constant source of inspiration for me. Your passion and dedication inspire me every day to dream bigger and work harder.

I would like to thank my wonderful wife, who gave me the gift of our two children, from the bottom of my heart. Despite the challenges of juggling your own business and a family, you manage to be extraordinarily successful at both. Your strength, wisdom and support are the beacon of light in my life.

Not forgetting my friends who have provided countless fulfilling conversations. Your perspectives, advice and friendship have enriched me immensely along the way.

This book is not only a product of my work, but also the result of the love, support and inspiration I have received from each of you. I am deeply grateful for every moment we have shared and for everything you have done to support me. Thank you for being a part of my journey.

About the author

Labinot Gashi has several years of experience in the areas of Google Ads, search engine optimization, remarketing, email marketing, online business development, online strategy, conversion optimization, mobile marketing and display marketing, artificial intelligence.

He also supports countless major clients in the areas of online marketing, performance, business development and many other areas.

Labinot Gashi also founded the luxury jewelry brand

MUAU (https://www.muau.ch , https://www.muau.com , https://www.eden-schmuck.ch together with his wife. He also sells the most expensive GOLD honey in the world with his brand AURMEL (https://www.aurmel.com).

He has already created and optimized over 100 websites and web stores in the luxury, automotive, sports, NGO, fashion, education and many other sectors.

Labinot Gashi is a lecturer at various universities and universities of applied sciences and is also on the board of directors of a children's foundation (https://www.Kinderstiftung.info).

Further training courses attended

Master in Digital Marketing

Google training (Google Ads, YouTube, analytics, display marketing, mobile marketing, user experience)

NLP (Neurolinguistic Programming)

NLS (Neurolinguistic Selling)

INFORMATION

All information contained in this book has been compiled to the best of our knowledge and belief. Nevertheless, errors cannot be completely ruled out. For this reason, the information contained in this book does not constitute any obligation or guarantee.

Notwithstanding the care taken in the preparation of text, illustrations and programs, and in view of the fast-moving nature of the industry, neither the publisher nor the author can accept any legal responsibility or liability for possible errors and their consequences. The common names, trade names, product designations etc. reproduced in this work may also be trademarks without special identification and as such are subject to the statutory provisions.

PREFACE

DIGITAL GOLD

100 digital business ideas: How to start your own online business

Imagine holding the key to your own digital empire. In an era where digital transformation is revolutionizing our world, this book offers you the blueprint for success.

Labinot Gashi, a seasoned pioneer in online business, shares his accumulated insights in "Digital Gold" and shows you how to start your own successful online business with 100 innovative digital business ideas. Whether you are just starting out or want to take your existing business to the next level, this book is your indispensable companion.

Get inspired and discover:

- **Proven Strategies:** From Google Ads to conversion optimization – use the secrets of digital marketing for your success.
- **Diverse Business Models:** From freemium to e-commerce – find the model that perfectly fits you and your vision.
- **Practical Guides:** Step-by-step methods to turn your ideas into reality and achieve sustainable growth.

- **Success Stories:** Learn from real examples and success stories that show you too can find your digital gold.

Each of the 100 business ideas is a potential treasure waiting to be discovered by you. Start your journey to financial independence and entrepreneurial success today. "Digital Gold" is more than a book – it's your starting shot into an exciting new future.

INTRODUCTION

Basic principle of the book

This book is intended to serve as inspiration and guidance for a possible business. True to the motto "inspiration first, then perspiration", the implementation of what you have learned is entirely up to you. I will show you different ways in which you can achieve your "digital gold".

Since we are now in the age of "googling" and the use of artificial intelligence such as ChatGPT, you can research in-depth questions on various topics yourself. There are at least a hundred tutorials on YouTube for every challenge and the AI is also a good help.

It is best to read through all the chapters that interest you and draw up an action plan while you are reading. That way you won't miss any important implementations.

What is your "Ikigai"?

The concept of "Ikigai" stems from Japanese culture and offers us a fascinating perspective on the meaning of life, the source of true joy and the ultimate goal in life. In its essence, it embodies the uplifting feeling of having a cause worth jumping out of bed for every morning with enthusiasm.

To prevent your venture from degenerating into a fleeting moment of inspiration and to prevent an initial challenge from throwing you off track, it is essential to explore your personal "ikigai". Why exactly do you aspire to start this particular business? What sparks your passion?

The awareness and deep connection to your "ikigai" will not only ignite an unwavering motivation within you, but also give you an almost superhuman stamina in the face of the inevitable challenges of entrepreneurship. Ready for weeks stretching over a hundred hours of work? With a clearly defined "Ikigai", such endeavors are not only doable, but also fulfilling.

Therefore, it is crucial to pause and reflect before you take the plunge: what is the deep, driving reason behind starting your new business? Recognize your "Ikigai" and you will hold the key to true fulfillment and lasting success in your hands.

Digital business models

The digital transformation is progressing inexorably in all areas of life. In particular, the constant availability of smartphones and thus mobile broadband connections means that we are all doing more and more everyday things in the digital space or with the help of corresponding tools or other products. This applies to both our private and business lives.

With this in mind, various business models have emerged and established themselves over the last 20 years that relate precisely to the requirements or expectations associated with increasing digitalization. For many people, it is now completely normal to use value creation approaches that are based entirely on digital technologies. It is now possible to open a bank account digitally, buy a car digitally, rent and let vacation accommodation digitally, do the weekly shop digitally or complete entire training courses digitally.

"My mother told me that thirty years ago, they thought it was impossible to talk to someone on the phone without a cable and even see each other. Today we simply call this phenomenon Facetime and can no longer imagine that it didn't exist."

But what constitutes such digital business models, what characteristics do they generally have and how do typical digital business ideas work? These and other questions will be answered in the following chapters.

In principle, a business model is digital if digital technologies have a fundamental influence on the way in which the respective company structures the way it does business and ultimately generates revenue. In this case, customer benefit is shaped centrally by digital processes. The core objective (as with other business models) is to create added value that customers are willing to pay for.

However, digital business approaches must not be seen as a mere digital extension of conventional businesses. The addition of digital technologies is not sufficient for a corresponding classification: This would be the case, for example, if an online store were to be set up as an additional sales channel for a stationary business. A genuine or completely digital business model, on the other hand, is almost completely located in the digital space.

This definition can be further clarified by the following typical characteristics of digital business approaches:

- Without the use of digital technologies, the value added would not be possible.
- Both customer acquisition and sales are based on digital channels - and both are often supported by digital automation.
- The products provided have a market and are purchased, which means that a monetizable, digital customer need can be served through the business models.
- Digital innovations often shape the respective business models - they are based on products or ideas that have not previously existed on the market in this form.

What do digital business models mean for society?

As already indicated at the beginning, digital is having a growing influence on all of our lives. In this context, digital business approaches often offer customers huge benefits from which they can profit (because they are digital) with relatively little effort. Such business models are usually particularly scalable for the companies concerned.

These two facts in particular are contributing massively to the fact that companies based on purely analog business models are coming under strong pressure. They are also trying to digitize their services and thus generate a similar level of customer acceptance and corresponding profit. In addition, it is increasingly becoming part of people's expectations to be able to at least digitally support certain or even more everyday to-dos. All of this is continuously driving the digital transformation.

Both current and future generations are growing up with digital business models and internalizing them, which increases their social relevance.

In this context, the term "digital natives" must be taken into account: This refers to the generations that have grown up with the strong digital development (from around 1980 onwards).They have no fear of contact with the digital world and therefore use its possibilities on a broad front. Digital businesses often focus on these target groups (or should do so for business success).

What do you need to pay particular attention to when introducing a digital business idea?

A digital business approach must first of all answer the same questions as a traditional business:

- What do we offer our customers?
- Who belongs to our target group?
- What is the best way to reach these people?
- In which (digital) way is the service provided?
- How do we generate sales?

Answering the above questions generates a wide range of information. This information can be collected, analyzed, evaluated and processed using digital technologies in order to ultimately ensure efficient implementation (and appropriate long-term operation).

The comprehensive use of relevant data and the associated digital tools is one of the main prerequisites for (sustained) digital business success.

Overview of typical digital business models

In the following chapters, examples of the successful implementation of digital business approaches and then specific business ideas in practice are presented. In addition to general explanations, the focus is also on monetization options, specific requirements for implementation and marketing tips.

First (before moving on to the business ideas), the following digital value creation approaches should be explained in more detail:

- Free model
- Freemium model
- On-demand model
- E-commerce model
- Marketplace model
- Ecosystem model
- Access-over-ownership model / sharing model
- Experience model
- Subscription model
- Open source model
- Hidden revenue generation model

Free model

(Advertising-supported model)

The free model: Free service for advertising revenue

In a free model, companies offer services or even goods free of charge. Prominent products of this digital business approach are used by many people every day: most search engines and social media platforms belong to this segment. Some of the best-known examples are Google, YouTube, Instagram, Facebook, Bing and TikTok. Numerous apps also make use of corresponding processes and their advantages. However, there is often a fine line between the free and premium models.

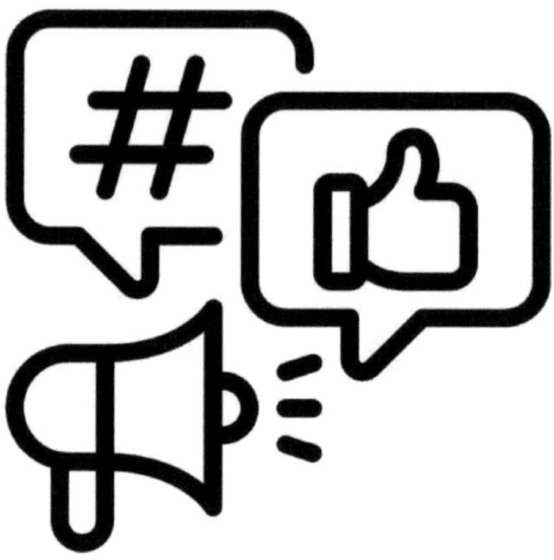

How can the free model be monetized?

Initially, free offers are often a loss-making business. Companies can only earn money with them once a certain number of users have been reached. At a certain point, the profit is finally greater than the costs and the free model begins to pay off.

The product becomes attractive for advertisers due to the continuously increasing number of users at best. Other companies should be persuaded to place advertisements in connection with the free offer. The operator is then paid for the relevant advertising space. Corresponding advertising partners should initially be recruited via good old direct acquisition. The promotion options should also be clearly communicated within the product. As soon as the number of customers or users is large enough, the advertising spaces will sell themselves.

In their book "Business Model Generation", business innovation experts Osterwalder and Pigneur propose the following priorities for free business models subsidized by advertising revenue:

- Customer groups: With a free model, companies should concentrate on addressing the largest possible customer groups in order to attract as many advertisers as possible.
- Value proposition: Value is created through the benefit of a free product or service. The resulting customer base creates the most important impulse for advertisers. The free offer must therefore convince users as much as possible with its added value.
- Sources of profit: Profit is primarily generated from advertisers who use the product for their promotions. Later, depending on the focus of the offer, additional paid services are also conceivable. In this case, the approach changes to a freemium model.
- Resources: Users are the most important resource. The greater the reach of the offer or the more people use it, the greater the revenue opportunities.
- Critical measures: In order to convince users in the long term, the product must be maintained and continuously developed. In this way, advertisers will continuously generate sales.
- Network: For a purposeful genesis, those responsible should focus on developing partnerships that can drive the offering forward. New ideas, additional features and greater usability will make it more attractive for users and therefore for advertisers.
- Costs: The management and development of the product as well as the generation of traffic cause the highest costs.

What requirements are important for the successful implementation of the free model?

In principle, it is relatively easy to distribute a free product and build a community for it (as long as it offers the target group real added value). However, comparatively large numbers of visitors or users are required for sustainability, which in turn is relatively difficult to achieve.

To create advantageous conditions, the product should ideally be truly innovative. If there are competitors, it must be able to compete with them in terms of its benefits, discoverability and originality. If the services offered within the free model are really good, the target persons will see them as beneficial.

To do this, you should first analyze your own company and the current market in the respective niche. It is important to get a clear overview of what the potential competition is offering for free and how your own product can do it better.

To maximize the potential of your offer, you should take a very close look at your own customers. Only if you deliver precisely the features that the target customers particularly expect in the respective application context will they accept the product. Ideally, users will be surprised with useful features that they are not familiar with. Unique selling points and, of course, optimal functionality will attract new interested parties and ultimately users.

Marketing and tips: How do you publicize the free model?

In principle, all channels with which the target group has regular contact should be used for publicity and for user and customer acquisition.

Especially with the free model, a good reputation is particularly valuable for the company in question. This is because many people initially assume that free offers are of lower quality, have a smaller range of functions or similar deficits. This impression can be refuted by deliberately honing the reputation.

In order to achieve optimal results, all employees of the company must be involved in improving the reputation. Precise communication rules are essential for this. A good reputation is one of those things that is hard to build and very easy to lose. A single wrong message or a misguided campaign can undo all the hard work.

FREEMIUM MODEL

The freemium model: Free basic features plus paid extras with great added value

The core of this digital business model is to grant customers or users access to a product free of charge, but only offer a certain amount of basic features or resources. Additional elements - usually extra functions with particularly high added value or extended (individual) services - that go beyond the basic tools are ultimately only available in a paid full version.

The term "freemium" is therefore made up of the terms "free" - for the free version - and "premium" - for the offer with the extended features.

This business approach is particularly common in the software world, but it is also widely used for online streaming platforms or other (mostly) digital services. All kinds of computer programs or mobile apps are made available using this model. Some very well-known products from this segment are Spotify, Google Drive, Dropbox, Slack and Xing.

How can the freemium model be monetized?

There are actually very different ways to monetize the freemium model. The trick is to offer basic functions or resources that appeal strongly to the respective target group on the one hand and then to integrate services on top that give these people special added value for which they are ultimately willing to pay.

Typical examples of freemium approaches or monetization variants that do just that are as follows:

- In so-called free-to-play computer games, revenue is generated through advertising placed in the game, which no longer appears in the premium version, and the sale of virtual items. In the latter context, players buy weapons, magic powers and other items that give them advantages.

- With typical application software (as an on-premise or SaaS solution), basic and premium versions generally differ in terms of functionality. If you want to do more with the respective program than the basic version allows, you have to pay for it.

- Online services, such as on-demand streamers or file hosters, use different approaches. Again, advertising can be hidden by paying, but the memory, usage time or program selection can also be extended.

- Many newspapers and books are now also available in the freemium model. In the digital world, certain content can easily be reserved for paying customers.

- Sometimes hardware is even marketed under the freemium approach. These providers initially provide extensive component information, plans and instructions free of charge. As soon as the broadest possible interest has been created, customers can either purchase the parts required to build the product themselves and get to work or have it assembled via an extended service. The focus is primarily on people who do not have the time or simply do not have the skills to do it themselves.

What requirements are important for a successful implementation of the freemium model?

Interested parties should at best surprise their target group and offer them paid solutions that not only optimally complement the freely available features, but which ideally are not available anywhere else in this quality.

The balance between the free and paid offerings must be right. This can be a major challenge, especially with new products for which there is no experience of user behavior.

- It can quickly happen that the free version allows too many features. As a result, relatively few users are likely to decide to purchase the full version.

- On the other hand, if the free service offers hardly any options, many potential customers see no point in testing it. The user numbers fall short of the actual potential.

Companies that use the freemium model should not be afraid to adapt their product if they realize that the free version either offers too much or that too much of the offer is behind the paywall.

Marketing and tips: How do you publicize the freemium model?

Ideally, demand is only generated by the product. A good example of this is the file host Dropbox: Before it or its service, which allows you to easily store all kinds of files online, existed, most people were unaware of the huge benefits of being able to easily access your documents, pictures, music, etc. from anywhere using internet-enabled devices. In this case, more storage means more flexibility and efficiency, which many people are happy to spend money on. In such a case, the freemium offer practically promotes and sells itself.

In addition, potential users and customers are generally particularly easy to reach with free products. If the respective offer does its job very well, it will be accepted by many people. If it even surprises users with its extended features, that alone is the best way to attract customers. The freemium model can therefore be seen as a marketing method in itself.

In this context, there is a very interesting quote from the CEO of Evernote: *"The easiest way to get a million people to pay for something is to get a billion people to use it."*

ON-DEMAND MODEL

Although the term "on-demand" has now been Germanized, it basically means "on demand" or "on call". The basic concept of the digital on-demand business model can already be explained perfectly with this translation: corresponding companies therefore provide their products precisely on demand.

The highlight here is that this often happens immediately (at least in the digital space) and that the (usually digital) services are generally only available for the exact period of time in which they are needed. This enables quick solutions to needs or problems on the one hand and cost savings on the other, as customers "borrow" instead of buying. However, the on-demand sector also includes businesses where goods are purchased on a long-term basis. They are then also provided immediately or at least with minimal time expenditure.

Typically, on-demand is used as a digital business model for streaming services such as Netflix or Amazon Prime. There are gradations of on-demand delivery, on-demand service, on-demand food, on-demand logistics and even on-demand manufacturing (although overlaps are possible).

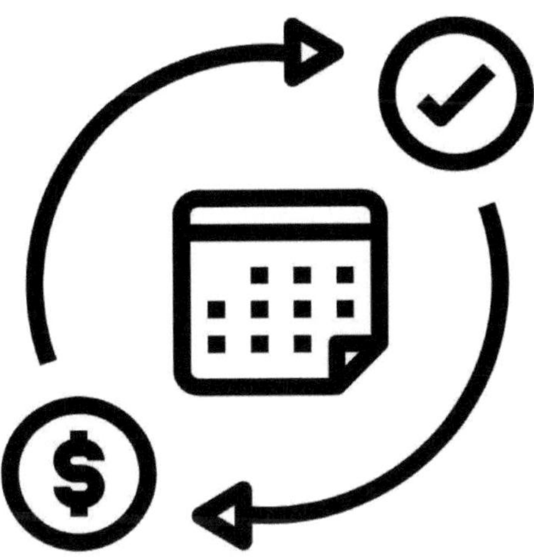

How can the on-demand model be monetized?

Anyone using on-demand as a digital business model is primarily selling products. There are two typical approaches:

1. Customers can buy or rent a good or service once.
2. Alternatively, they can take out a subscription, which they then use to make regular calls.

The individual levels of the on-demand model are the best way to explain what can be offered and within what framework.

- **On-demand provision:** In this form, digital products such as music

(Spotify) or literature (Amazon Prime) are usually provided directly on demand. Subscription monetization is common.

- **Service-on-demand:** This on-demand approach often refers to services that are not only requested in the digital space, but also serve concerns located there. For example, it is possible to hire web design freelancers online via Upwork. Service-on-demand can also be transferred to the real world - for example, rides can be booked promptly via the Uber app. The corresponding services are normally billed once.

- **Food-on-demand:** Companies such as UberEats or Instacart offer interested parties the opportunity to buy food on-demand and have it delivered quickly. Here you either pay individually or take out a subscription.

- **On-demand logistics:** on-demand logistics works in a similar way to food-on-demand, except that all kinds of goods are delivered or transported in the shortest possible time, regardless of a specific online store offer. There are several services that offer this type of service, particularly in the USA. Payment is generally made individually.

- **On-demand production:** On-demand manufacturing is primarily about having products that are normally only produced in large quantities manufactured individually, even in small quantities. Many of the steps required for such an order are carried out digitally or online. There is great potential here in 3D printing.

What requirements are important for the successful implementation of the on-demand model?

At a very basic level, the products offered for distribution in an on-demand model need to be uncomplicated and quick to provide. In principle, this would be possible with any product or service (which on-demand manufacturing in particular has proven time and again). But it should pay off.

If on-demand is an option, the timely delivery of orders or the prompt completion of other pending tasks must be guaranteed. This is the only way to meet general expectations and build a satisfied customer base in this model. Especially when selling physical products, delivery partners must be able to eliminate delays and ensure that orders can always be fulfilled on time.

Quality must not suffer in any way. It is important to remember that customers who use on-demand services generally expect very fast and convenient results. In the event of problems, a solution must be found reliably and promptly.

In general, it is important to make the on-demand offer as easily accessible as possible for new and existing customers. Today, this definitely includes a broad coverage of digital media. Optimizing apps and websites is a must. Last but not least, an ideal on-demand business model simplifies communication between customers and vendors.

Marketing and tips: How do you publicize the on-demand model?

One of the core objectives of the on-demand business model is to provide potential buyers with solutions in the moment. Such prompt processes have always marked an elementary customer need: being able to get everything immediately and without great effort (in many cases without leaving their own four walls) at any time of the day or night still feels downright magical to customers. Anyone who creates such feelings with their on-demand model is engaging in powerful marketing through this alone.

Nevertheless, well-known approaches to customer acquisition and retention should of course not be dispensed with. Digital measures such as search engine optimization, SEA, social media marketing, etc. should be given special consideration here. After all, people who want or need something on-demand and therefore usually promptly obtain information online just as quickly and easily.

E-COMMERCE MODEL

The e-commerce model: selling goods or services online with great potential

E-commerce is still the most successful digital business model. It is also the oldest approach to earning money on the Internet. In its basic form, tangible goods are sold to consumers via an online store.

However, there are a few other forms that have received increasing attention in recent years. For example, digital products such as software or e-books can of course also be sold online - and more and more services can also be booked digitally. In addition to B2C sales, the number of B2B online stores is growing steadily.

A distinction is generally made between pure e-commerce companies and hybrid stores, i.e. those that support their bricks-and-mortar business with an online store (or vice versa). Meanwhile, the boundaries between traditional sales and online sales are becoming blurred in many cases thanks to options such as click-and-collect.

How can the e-commerce model be monetized?

Monetization is comparatively clear in this digital business approach: income is generated through online sales of goods or services. However, there are various business models available for this, into which e-commerce is fundamentally divided and which offer very different potentials.

- **Business-to-Consumer (B2C):** In this "classic" form of online retail, consumers purchase items over the Internet for their own use.
- **Business-to-Business (B2B):** In B2B e-commerce, companies sell goods or services online to other companies.
- **Consumer-to-Consumer (C2C):** C2C is comparable to a flea market or an auction on the internet, where private individuals sell goods to each other. C2C e-commerce companies provide corresponding platforms.

- **Consumer-to-business (C2B):** In C2B e-commerce, private individuals or (potential) customers create value for companies. This approach can be seen, for example, in review portals or platforms for stock photography, where images are offered by non-professionals for business purposes.
- **Business-to-Government (B2G):** When a private company sells goods or services online to a public institution, this is B2G e-commerce business.

What requirements are important for the successful implementation of the e-commerce model?

At a very basic level, it is important to find out whether the respective target group has any significant interest in purchasing the goods offered online and whether sales on the Internet are possible in principle. In most cases, both of these questions can be answered in the affirmative: In fact, almost all products can be sold digitally in some form and pretty much every prospective customer today is primarily looking for options that enable challenges or needs to be solved directly via the web.

Ideally, something is also offered that is not available anywhere else in this form or in this scope of provision.

Data is also one of the most important foundations for successful e-commerce activities. This allows precise target group and competitor segmentation to be carried out. Finally, they give e-commerce businesses the opportunity to utilize best practices in customer acquisition and retention, especially targeted marketing and marketing automation. If you want to fully exploit the potential of digital sales, you should definitely take a close look at the many ways in which data can be used.

However, before the power of data can be used on a broad front and in the long term, extensive research must be carried out (in which data is also collected, of course). The focus here should be on the largest competitors or the market in the relevant segment and the target group that is ultimately expected to buy the products on offer.

E-commerce operators need to find out what products other stores offer, where and to what extent they are present online (social media, marketplaces, review portals, etc.), what the unique selling points of their business are, and so on. These analyses provide companies with elementary clues for the efficient launch of their digital business: from choosing a name with high recognition value to determining the perfect goods or services and effective marketing measures.

In order to study your own target group, it is best to contact people in your personal company or customer network directly. Ideally, professional surveys are carried out, which may then identify e-commerce gaps that you can fill with your own offers.

Marketing and tips: How do you publicize the e-commerce model?

One very important e-commerce marketing tip has already been mentioned: The efficient use of data often makes all the difference. Data can be used in almost every area of (digital) customer acquisition and retention. It makes sense to start with the basics of inbound marketing.

With appropriate strategies, people can be very effectively encouraged to recognize a brand and even attribute expert status to it in their field: the best prerequisites for strong long-term business relationships.

Content marketing or blogging, email and social media and, last but not least, SEO and SEA are the core elements that every e-commercer should have on their agenda for customer acquisition or retention. The target group and their problems or wishes that need to be solved with their own offers must always remain in focus.

MARKETPLACE MODEL

(PEER-TO-PEER, TWO-SIDED MARKETPLACE)

The marketplace model: simple sales for retailers with high traction potential

When companies use the marketplace model as a digital business approach, they generally do so by providing other companies or private individuals with a space on the internet where they can offer their products. Specialized e-commerce sites form the foundation. Many retailers generally register on such platforms and (ideally) gain numerous advantages: good marketplaces primarily provide improved reach and features that make it easy for sellers to make their offers available, findable and advertised online.

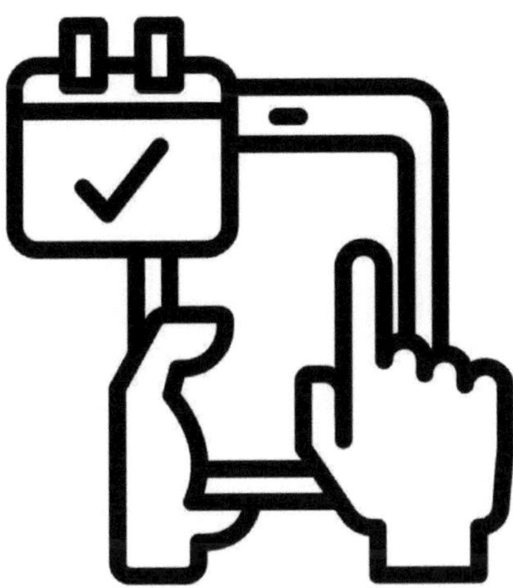

The big difference to the conventional e-commerce model is that a marketplace brings together the product range of several sellers and not just the stock of a single seller.

This digital business model is divided into two basic functionalities:

- **Vertical marketplaces:** Products in a specific category are offered on a vertical marketplace. A typical example is Uber, on whose platform only passenger transportation services are sold.
- **Horizontal marketplaces:** A horizontal marketplace, on the other hand, is much broader. The range on offer here can include a wide variety of goods or services. A mixture of digital and tangible items is also possible. The most famous examples of this type of marketplace are Amazon and eBay.

There are also special B2C and B2B marketplaces. Some marketplace operators also allow private individuals to sell via their platforms - as already mentioned at the beginning. Some solutions are even designed primarily for private sales (C2C) - such as (eBay) classified ads.

In principle, marketplaces are conceivable for all types of products.

How can the marketplace model be monetized?

There are three main ways for companies to monetize a marketplace, which can be used in combination.

- **Sale of merchant spaces:** Merchants generally pay to be allowed to offer their products on a marketplace. A commission model based on sales is typical.
- **Own use of the "sales area":** Companies that provide a marketplace sometimes also do so in order to bring their own goods or services to their target group. In such cases, the sales platform is usually an additional source of income to conventional sales.
- **Advertising revenue:** Last but not least, marketplaces always offer companies the opportunity to sell advertising space. This can relate to classic banners on the one hand, but also to ads that allow sellers to place certain products more prominently in the rankings. The more established a platform is, the more profitable the advertising business becomes.

What requirements are important for the successful implementation of the marketplace model?

People interested in specific types of goods or services now actually prefer to start their search on the relevant marketplaces - regardless of the type of product in question. The usually large selection in combination with reviews, recommendations, sorting, etc. is a strong argument in favor of such platforms. For marketplace operators, this means that they should, on the one hand, combine a comprehensive range of products and, on the other hand, make the items easy to find using a powerful search function with all the expected filters.

On a technical level, the APIs, i.e. the interfaces, are crucial: only with the right connections can retailers integrate their products quickly and easily - time is money. Special modules for payment processing, order management, offer creation and discounting should be precisely tailored by the marketplace operator to the typical needs of the targeted providers and their target group. Correspondingly feature-rich and, in the best case, individually customizable systems offer ideal opportunities for rapid scalability: and this is exactly what many marketplace stakeholders particularly want.

Marketing and tips: How do you publicize the marketplace model?

Marketplaces and retailers interested in marketplace sales no longer focus exclusively on the purchasing process. Sellers are usually aware of the potential benefits of this form of sales and expect a marketplace to serve them comprehensively. This starts with product presentation and extends to specific brand building, customer reviews and advertisements. The more opportunities there are to steadily increase the conversion rate, the better.

Product and merchant review features in particular are becoming increasingly important for sellers on marketplaces. Buyers are increasingly relying on corresponding reviews. They are therefore often a decisive factor for companies potentially offering their goods or services when choosing a product or market-place.

It is still extremely important for retailers to showcase their products perfectly and provide their customers with lots of appealing information about their items. Spaces for good and detailed product images and descriptions are therefore also an absolute must-have. Ideally, there is a shop-in-shop option that allows companies to have their very own e-commerce area on the platform. Individual designs support brand building and brand awareness.

By integrating these and, ideally, all other benefits demanded by the relevant target group, awareness of the respective marketplace system in its segment practically increases by itself. Nevertheless, "classic" marketing measures should of course not be omitted.

ECOSYSTEM MODEL

The ecosystem model: optimally serving customers in different areas and benefiting from strong growth

Marketing and tips: How do you publicize the ecosystem model?

Digital ecosystems offer companies enormous opportunities. More and more managers actually want to use the diverse possibilities for their own purposes: Various network effects and participation in the business of others offer the prospect of future-proof positioning in one's own domain.

However, building a digital ecosystem is extremely challenging. This is primarily due to the complexity of numerous integrated technologies, companies and (human) resources that need to be mastered, as well as the fact that new terrain typically needs to be explored and the associated uncertainty.

Nevertheless, a digital ecosystem needs to enter the market quickly and grow if it is to be successful. This is because the competition is fierce and is constantly growing in many areas. More and more companies are being inspired by the success stories of Amazon and co. and are looking for their niches. Winning the race against the competition requires enormous manpower, initiative and courage as well as a sophisticated marketing strategy that is individually tailored to the respective company and customer requirements.

Access-over-ownership

Model / Sharing model

The access-over-ownership model: renting instead of selling and scoring points with automation plus personality

The access-over-ownership model is also sometimes referred to as the sharing model. The latter term illustrates the principles of this digital business approach particularly well. This is because companies that offer access products actually share them with their customers in a certain way: The goods or machines, cars, bicycles or even apartments, business premises and entire industrial plants provided are not sold, but rented out. The organization and brokerage of such goods is generally carried out via the Internet.

This principle of sharing has been around for some time, but it has been reinvented by the advance of digitalization, making it more convenient, faster and ultimately more effective. Today, it is very easy to temporarily book (almost) all kinds of things that are needed for everyday life or business purposes. Specialized services and apps such as Airbnb (vacation apartments),

Regus (offices), Flinkey (vehicles) or Toolbot (tools) make this possible. *These applications and Access-Over-Ownership in general are characterized by a high degree of automation.*

How can the access-over-ownership model be monetized?

One major advantage of the access-over-ownership model - if done correctly - is its clear contribution to sustainability: by renting out properties, they are better utilized and fewer new products of the same type need to be manufactured or disposed of. Nevertheless, this approach is of course not only dedicated to the "good cause".

For the operators of such platforms, sharing is primarily for economic reasons: In fact, it is possible to profit on a broad front here. This is because products are generally relatively inexpensive to rent (especially in the digital space), which is why they are used relatively frequently. Once such a business is established, it can be scaled almost indefinitely.

Of course, the companies primarily generate their income through rents or usage fees. However, they can also receive sales commissions from any third-party providers brought on board or advertising revenue. In addition, lucrative sharing platforms are currently sought-after investment objects for investors.

What requirements are important for the successful implementation of the access-over-ownership model?

First of all, products must be available that allow sales via Access-Over-Ownership and guarantee efficient marketing in the long term. Ideally, these should be high-quality, durable goods that are used regularly, but whose purchase represents a disproportionately high investment for most people. At best, there is no such sharing approach in the respective segment.

If these requirements are met, it is particularly important to ensure that the **user experience** is kept high. This plays a major role in the success of the sharing model. To improve the user's experience when interacting with the product, it is worth considering the following points:

- **Cooperation with the community:** With the access-over-ownership model, continuous feedback from a community is extremely important. On the one hand, it promotes sales if it is published. On the other hand, it can make your own offers even better. It is important to accept praise or criticism and implement it where possible. Taking direct user concerns into account gives buyers the impression that they have a certain amount of control, which promotes customer loyalty.
- **Smooth processes:** The smoother the sharing process runs, the happier the users are. Access Over Ownership companies that provide their customers with a worry-free experience and eliminate as many weak points in the process as possible are therefore proving to be

particularly successful.

- **Staying human and personal:** New technologies and digital business approaches are fascinating. They often offer the opportunity to achieve a lot quickly with little effort. This is also the case with the access-over-ownership model. Most of the processes typically associated with this are automated. Nevertheless, a personal connection to the brand in question should always be supported as much as possible. If you manage to combine automation and personality in the best possible way, you not only trigger the practical needs of your customers, but also their emotions - and as we all know, this can be extremely beneficial for business.

Marketing and tips: How do you publicize the access-over-ownership model?

Anyone wishing to use the access-over-ownership model for their own purposes should of course first and foremost ensure that the corresponding rental processes run smoothly and that the products on offer are of a high quality. At the same time, it is important to establish an effective and easy-to-use evaluation system.

This is because genuine customer reviews have particularly strong traction in the context of this digital business approach. The main reason for this is that sharing products are often used for critical applications: For example, a rented car must not only be fast and reliable, but also guarantee its driver adequate safety for life and limb. Vacations often stand or fall on the attractiveness of vacation apartments. Or let's take a chartered industrial plant - if it doesn't work smoothly, enormous sums of money are quickly lost.

Positive comments from real customers in such or similar contexts create significantly more trust than any advertising, no matter how honest. They will bring many more prospective customers.

Experience model

The experience model: experiences and emotions for more sales and strong long-term loyalty

When companies use the experience model, they provide products that deliver experiences that would not be possible without digital technologies. The positive experience itself is not necessarily at the heart of the business activity, but is a key value in this. It can relate to very different goods or services.

Purchase decisions between comparable products (in saturated markets) can be pushed very effectively through (ideally) strong emotionalization. In addition to the pure offer functionality, customers are sold a larger world of experience, which in the digital context is often based on online opportunities that create outstanding added value and unique selling points. This creates an emotional and therefore very strong differentiation from (similar) competitor products.

Many large corporations use the experience approach as a digital business model in various forms. This includes Tesla in particular, where digital services and even a digital ecosystem are integrated into the cars. This brings special digital experiences to the products that did not previously exist to this extent in the automotive industry.

How can the experience model be monetized?

The experience model is monetized through sales of the products with which the relevant experiences are brought to customers. The more positive and unique the experiences are, the more sales can be generated with the goods or services.

The key to successfully using this approach is emotionalization.

- Customers today are no longer "only" attracted by good functionality. They want to find personality, trust and other emotional values.
- If everything is done correctly here, this will ultimately result in more effective buyer acquisition and retention.
- Consumers in particular are very willing not only to buy products

that convey certain feelings and experiences, but also to spend more money on them and to make such purchases again and again - if necessary or desirable.

What requirements are important for the successful implementation of the Experience Model?

At the very base, the product being sold must allow for an additional digital experience. However, this is actually possible in almost every sales context today. In the simplest case, apps and other digital helpers can support the performance or usability of a wide range of goods or services and thus create special experiences.

The key here is to use digital influences to create experiences that deliver real added value and are unique at best. It is true that the experience model can also be used if you simply offer the digital extensions that all companies in the respective segment provide. In this case, however, the approach falls far short of its potential.

Ideally, we should dig deep into the usage habits and expectations of shoppers to uncover hidden potential. Finally, a close link between the products and personal marketing and service innovations or specific activities that affect the respective experiences is necessary. Ideally, the offering and the digital experience will literally merge and become inseparable in the minds of users.

Marketing and tips: How do you publicize the Experience model?

In order for the experience model to create the desired experiences, it is important to take as personal an approach as possible in marketing. In general, companies should focus on the requirements, wishes and expectations of their typical customer base when acquiring and retaining customers. On the other hand, customers are increasingly looking for personal, close and direct interaction.

In the context of publicizing the experience model, these values and the adoption of corresponding tactics are even more relevant. For the most successful companies with this business approach, the digital experience of the offerings already begins in marketing and the measures implemented there.

Experience marketing and experiential marketing are important keywords here. In line with the experience model, experience campaigns offer the opportunity to make a tangible and lasting impression on potential buyers, to arouse genuine interest and, last but not least, to motivate people emotionally to share their experiences with relatives, friends and colleagues.

SUBSCRIPTION MODEL

The subscription model: regular income for stable and predictable sales

More and more companies are using a subscription model to bring their products to buyers. The most well-known representatives offering this business approach in the digital space include Netflix, Spotify, Apple, Microsoft and Amazon.

They all provide digital products on a regular basis and benefit from recurring revenue in return. The services are usually paid for monthly or annually. They can be flexibly utilized or adjusted depending on the focus of the offer.

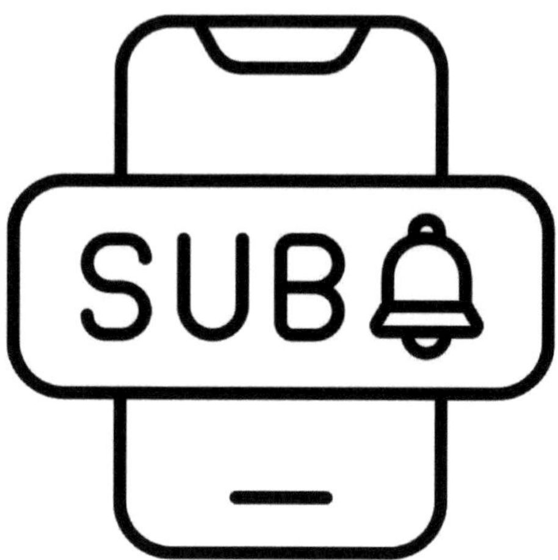

How can the subscription model be monetized?

The great advantage of the subscription model is that (if implemented wisely) it generates reliable and regular income. Companies have the opportunity to generate stable and predictable revenue. Customers are happy to accept such services because they usually mean increased convenience.

The basis of monetization is often less the sale of goods in the form of a complete transfer, but rather provision on demand. This digital business approach therefore has parallels with the on-demand model.

How the business ultimately works depends largely on the type of subscription. In the digital context, the following three types in particular can be distinguished.

- **The product subscription:** Customers generally purchase digital consumer products such as films or music, but also software on a subscription basis. These can then often be accessed on demand. In addition to providing these products, the respective company also takes care of hosting and offers a platform via which the services can be conveniently accessed.

- **The service subscription:** In the digital context, this subscription variant often refers to social networks or software providers. Additional services can then be booked with the relevant companies via regular payments. Examples include LinkedIn Premium or extended support for business systems.
- **The e-commerce subscription:** With digital subscriptions of this kind, the boundaries to transactions with tangible products or services in the physical world are sometimes blurred. Consumers or business customers can use special apps to secure offers or benefits. For example, Deutsche Bahn offers the opportunity to use train tickets as a subscription via a mobile application.

What requirements are important for the successful implementation of the subscription model?

Subscription models are generally associated with a higher purchasing hurdle compared to one-off purchases. Companies that want to take advantage of this digital business approach need to be aware of this. After all, the customer is well aware that taking out a subscription means ongoing costs. For this reason, the products in question should generally provide very high added value, which should ideally be made particularly clear by offering them as a subscription. The price should also appear as attractive as possible.

It is important to make the onboarding process quick and easy. If there are pitfalls in the way, it is relatively likely that customers who question their purchases more than others will reconsider and ultimately decide against the subscription. In this context, the following situation is extremely important: various studies have come to the conclusion that a significant number of potential buyers are not prepared to complete a registration process that takes longer than ten minutes of their time.

Marketing and tips: How do you publicize the subscription model?

Subscriptions require special attention in marketing due to their relatively high purchase hurdle and the fact that it is naturally desirable to retain subscribers beyond a contract period. In order to build up a strong appeal, companies should personalize their offers as much as possible and advertise them in an equally differentiated way. Usage data from long-term customer relationships can be automatically analyzed for preferences with the help of AI systems and promotions can be tailored accordingly.

Investments in customized customer centricity are very profitable in the long term. It is not only a way of attracting buyers, but also of retaining them through continuous measures. The latter is the basic prerequisite for a successful long-term subscription approach.

The key for new customers is often the offer of a test phase: by initially granting free access to the respective products, the target group can immediately convince themselves of their quality. The most attractive keyword for potential customers is "free". If something costs nothing, users don't take any risks. Once they have registered and experienced the added value in practice, they are relatively likely to stay.

OPEN SOURCE MODEL

The open source model: collaborative and decentralized software development for more attention and investors

In the context of digital business models, the open source model primarily refers to the distribution of software products. The source code of these programs is publicly available, can be viewed without restriction and can ultimately also be freely adapted.

Corresponding solutions are (further) developed collaboratively and decentrally on the basis of these prerequisites. In principle, everyone can contribute and benefit from the input and skills of others. Some of the most famous products or companies that use open source are WordPress, Mozilla Firefox, Linux, MySQL, Gimp and LibreOffice.

Nowadays, work on and the associated development of open source software generally takes place via specialized platforms. The systems are hosted on these platforms and innovations or relevant suggestions from contributors are bundled. The best-known addresses include GitHub and GitLab. This is where all relevant changes come together and are then implemented or not, depending on the issue.

How can the open source model be monetized?

In many cases, open source products are not sold directly. They are made available free of charge so that as many people as possible can contribute to their further development. However, this does not have to be the case: The term "open source" does not necessarily refer to the fact that something is available for free, but rather to the fact that the source code of the product in question is made freely accessible and publicly viewable.

Some open source software projects offer both free and paid versions or additional services. There are a variety of monetization opportunities with such offers. In detail, this often involves additional functions, extended support, specific training or other outstanding added value. For example, the basic version of software can be freely available, while variants that have already been optimized by the community are made available for a fee.

There is also the opportunity to monetize an open source product through third parties: On the one hand, this could be achieved via advertisements, for example. On the other hand, partner companies can be acquired to equip the open source solution with add-ons, for which commissions are then paid to users.

What requirements are important for a successful implementation of the open source model?

Quite a few open source projects are quite simple and streamlined. They are relatively simple helpers for everyday private or business tasks. Although some of them are widely used, as the solutions serve manageable task areas, only a few developers usually come up with the ideas and users are hardly willing to pay anything for them.

The commercial success of using the open source model is more likely if the resulting software helps to solve complex and challenging problems. The interest of potential buyers and specialists is therefore also increased. These groups of people then support the project through purchases or provide advice and develop useful extensions.

Software is often particularly interesting if it can be used in connection with a company's business-critical data and optimizes the relevant processes. However, there are countless other areas of application in which a correspondingly valuable product could be developed.

As a rule, however, this does not work without expert support, advice, licensing and long-term legal and marketing support.

Marketing and tips: How do you publicize the open source model?

Many typical marketing strategies that are generally aimed at users of software solutions can be used for customer acquisition and retention in connection with open source products.

With this digital business model, however, it is also important to ideally address potential partners or people who further develop the offered system and ultimately ensure its monetization. Optimal product coverage and communication on the major open source development platforms is particularly useful here to publicize the corresponding offers.

In addition, specific B2B marketing measures and requirements are usually helpful. They can be used to attract partner companies that support the open source project financially, for example through advertising or extensions for which commissions are paid. The business customer market, which is the focus of such marketing activities, is structured differently to its private customer counterpart. In some cases, there are very different conditions with regard to the effectiveness of individual marketing strategies.

The fact that there are many customers on the B2C market who make an immediate purchase decision is particularly striking. In the B2B market, on the other hand, it is generally not a single person in charge who decides whether to support an open source product - in this case. It is often several people who take care of the opportunities and risks of a possible entry as part of a longer-term consultation. This takes a relatively long time simply because of the many people involved and requires special persuasion approaches. In addition, the probable complexity of the solution on offer also contributes to the fact that companies do not make a decision immediately.

Due to the usually very specific type of product, B2B marketing does not tend to address the anonymous mass market. The number of market participants is usually smaller and their identity is often known. As a result, the individual requirements of potential partners can and should be incorporated very precisely into the marketing.

HIDDEN-REVENUE-GENERATION MODEL

(HIDDEN BUSINESS MODELS)

The hidden revenue generation model: diverse but sometimes complex revenue opportunities for maximized sales

As the name suggests, the hidden revenue generation model utilizes hidden opportunities for (mostly) additional revenue.

This digital business approach can be perfectly combined with others. This can be done, for example, by financing open source software through paid extensions or modules from third parties and related commissions, or by offering advertising space for sale on an e-commerce platform.

The products offered in the main store can sometimes be offered at a lower price or even completely free of charge through appropriate measures.

Prime examples of successful hidden revenue generation businesses are Google, Mozilla, Amazon and Apple.

How can the hidden revenue generation model be monetized?

In the hidden revenue generation, there are two basic orientations that also affect the potential for monetization.

1. **Pure hidden revenue generation:** In this case, the product sold does not generate any revenue per se. It is monetized exclusively through hidden revenues.

2. **The hybrid hidden revenue generation:** Here, the product itself - for example software - is sold and additional hidden revenue is generated - for example through commissions by connecting third-party modules.

What requirements are important for the successful implementation of the hidden revenue generation model?

With this digital business model, there are of course countless different conditions and associated strategic opportunities. However, for those who want to be as successful as possible, the following generally applies: Provide the greatest possible added value for all parties involved so that the hidden revenue generation model or the product in question is used extensively.

Google, probably the largest and highest-turnover hidden revenue generation business of all, is an excellent example of this premise. How has Google managed to become so successful (financially)? The answer lies in a convincing value proposition for three important stakeholders.

1. **User:** You can find an answer to "everything". Google is the most powerful search engine in the world. Thanks to its outstanding algorithm called PageRank, it was able to establish itself relatively soon after its launch at the end of the 1990s. Initially, it was not clear how the company would earn money. However, the founders wanted to ensure one thing: The engine should be free for its users. Today, it is gaining in quality year after year, day after day and hour after hour thanks to user data. In fact, it is the billions of people who use Google every day who make the search engine better and better through their input and data. Google uses this information to optimize its search algorithm so that it answers search queries more and more precisely, which in turn brings more and more users, who in turn pay with their interaction.

2. **Company:** They achieve more sales through targeted ads. Google uses a business model for advertising in which companies can participate in an advertising network called Ads. Advertisers can bid on keywords (such as "car rental") to have their goods or services displayed prominently when they are entered. Payment is based on clicks and the relevance of the individual advertising keyword. The more often the respective word is searched for and the more clicks

there are on the ad in question, the more expensive it is for advertisers. However, since the latter can generally draw the attention of many people to their offers in this way, this deal is worthwhile. It is an absolutely compelling value proposition that reliably drives up Google's profits. However, there is another important piece of the puzzle - the publishers.

3. **Publishers:** They benefit from easy monetization of their content. Millions of new articles are published on the Internet every day. This is not least due to the fact that information can now be marketed extremely profitably. Google's powerful algorithm indexes the entire visible web and accurately filters out the best content for all possible search queries. The more added value publishers create per search, the more likely it is that their content will appear at the top of the search engine rankings. This can be particularly worthwhile for publishers, as they have the opportunity to "rent" part of their websites to Google in order to place banners from companies in the Ads network, among other things. As soon as users browse the pages with the banners and click on them, the publishers turn their content into money. Google benefits from increased ad revenue and, in the case of really first-class content or correspondingly helpful suggestions in the search, from more and more users.

Marketing and tips: How do you publicize the hidden revenue generation model?

The major challenge in publicizing a hidden revenue generation approach lies in the fact that several stakeholders generally need to be addressed in the best possible way. Regardless of whether it is a hybrid variant or stand-alone hidden revenue, the product itself needs to be promoted on a small scale and the additional investors need to be kept on board.

There is a long way to go before a system as differentiated as that of Google, Amazon or other giants in this segment is achieved. However, only those who pull out all the stops right from the start will have the greatest possible success. Ideally, the target groups are addressed individually and based on a specific marketing strategy. Search engine optimization, content marketing, social media marketing, advertising - both B2C and B2B: all this and more can be helpful and even necessary.

Getting hidden revenue right is a highly complex matter - and so is customer acquisition and retention.

Business ideas

Turning digital business models into reality with the right business ideas

Now that we have highlighted the most important digital business models, the logical question is how to translate them into concrete business ideas? Whether you are a large company or a freelancer, this is a major challenge for anyone who wants to gain a foothold in the digital space.

The implementation of an extensive ecosystem model or a complex hidden revenue generation approach is generally not up for discussion to begin with. Especially in e-commerce, on-demand services, in connection with the optimization of experiences or in terms of (subscription-based) provision of added value information, there are good opportunities for prompt and lucrative long-term business.

Even freelancers or the smallest companies can get started relatively easily and quickly in these areas. Central business ideas that are generally particularly suitable for such groups are presented in more detail in the following chapters.

100 DIGITAL BUSINESS IDEAS

There are currently countless business opportunities that are realistic to implement. Human business creativity is limitless. In the following list, you will find 100 digital business ideas. We will focus on individual, exciting variants in the book and explain them in more detail.

1. E-learning platform
2. Online course marketplace
3. Virtual event planning
4. Digital marketing consultant
5. SEO consulting
6. E-commerce website
7. Dropshipping business
8. Affiliate marketing website
9. Blogging with advertising revenue
10. Influencer marketing agency
11. Social media management service

12. Virtual assistant services
13. Content creation and distribution
14. App development
15. Web design and development
16. Graphic design services
17. Podcast production
18. Youtube channel
19. Online photo sales
20. Stock music sale
21. E-book publisher
22. Audiobook production
23. Online coaching
24. Virtual fitness classes
25. Online nutritional advice
26. Telemedicine services
27. Online psychological counseling
28. Virtual interior design
29. 3D printing services
30. AI-based app development
31. IoT services
32. Cloud computing services

33. Data analysis consulting
34. Cybersecurity consulting
35. Blockchain-based projects
36. Cryptocurrency investment platform
37. Virtual accounting services
38. Online legal advice
39. Digital project management
40. Crowdfunding consulting
41. Online Public Relations
42. Virtual trade fair and exhibition platforms
43. Digital art gallery
44. Music production online
45. Digital fashion platform
46. Virtual reality experiences
47. Online gaming platform
48. Esports organization
49. Cloud gaming service
50. Game development
51. Travel planning website
52. Online travel agency
53. Virtual city tours

54. Language learning app
55. Translation services
56. Localization services
57. Virtual real estate viewings
58. Real estate management software
59. Online mortgage advice
60. Peer-to-peer lending platform
61. FinTech applications
62. Personal Finance Management app
63. Digital fundraising campaigns
64. Sustainability consulting online
65. Online community for sustainable practices
66. Digital second-hand store
67. Online upcycling workshops
68. Energy efficiency consulting
69. Virtual garden design
70. Online agricultural advice
71. Digital animal health advice
72. Pet care app
73. Online pet supplies store
74. Virtual pet sitting service

75. Online childcare
76. Virtual parenting aids
77. E-learning for children
78. Digital parenting advice
79. Online children's entertainment
80. Digital art and craft courses
81. Online cooking courses
82. Virtual wine tours
83. Online grocery market
84. Delivery service for healthy meals
85. Digital recipe platform
86. Virtual restaurant guides
87. Online catering coordination
88. Digital event management
89. Online ticket sales
90. Virtual concerts
91. Streaming service for movies/series
92. Digital book clubs
93. Online discussion forums
94. Virtual exhibitions
95. Digital learning games

96. Edutainment apps
97. Online mentoring platforms
98. Career advice online
99. Virtual job fairs
100. Remote working solutions

Our focus

As already mentioned, in this book we focus on a selection of digital business ideas. Entrepreneurial creativity lies in the implementation. This means that digital business ideas can also be implemented in combination with each other.

Surveys

Answering surveys as a digital business idea: diverse opportunities, but relatively low earnings

You can actually earn money by answering surveys. Depending on the effort and frequency with which the corresponding surveys are processed, additional income is possible. This digital business idea is therefore primarily aimed at freelancers or employees who want to build up a side income.

This is usually done via specialized platforms on the Internet. You register there and are then given access to surveys that precisely match your own interests or professional or specialist experience. Entscheider Club, Marketagent, Ampuls.ch, Ask GFK Schweiz, Opinio Helvetia, Mobrog and Atta Poll are large, frequently used addresses.

What is the market like for surveys?

Genuine, honest opinions are extremely important to companies! The survey as a means of gathering information about experiences and expectations in connection with goods or services sometimes has a somewhat outdated reputation compared to modern digital monitoring and analysis options. However, it still absolutely fulfills its purpose.

With the help of such surveys, companies can obtain very direct and ideally genuine, honest attitudes from their target groups towards their offers. Such data is extremely helpful in times when it is becoming increasingly important to ensure an all-round good user or customer experience. Most modern target group analyses or tracking methods only allow assumptions to be made about what (potential) buyers think about your products. Real customer opinions from surveys, on the other hand, provide a much more direct and reliable picture of the situation.

In addition to measurable and targeted information, it is important that (potential) customers who take part in a survey and who are also asked for their opinions by the company feel understood. Ideally, they will see their suggestions taken into account in the respective business development - especially in the relevant offers. This promotes both customer acquisition and long-term customer loyalty.

This means that, week after week and day after day, many surveys in a wide range of categories are posted on the major platforms. For freelancers, this means a lot of potential to earn money.

How can you earn money with the survey idea?

Those who earn money with surveys usually do so via specific online portals, as already mentioned at the beginning.

Here, companies place surveys with little effort, which they often use to support their market research, product optimization or quality assurance measures. However, surveys can also be set up in many other segments, such as environmental protection. It is just as easy for users to give their opinion. After registering, participants sometimes even receive suitable surveys by e-mail.

Payment is generally based primarily on the effort required to answer the respective questions. Some quick evaluations only earn a few centimes, others can earn ten or even more Swiss francs. Often the earnings are not calculated directly, but via a points system: For example, 3,000 survey points can equal 30 francs.

Hard-working survey participants earn 300 to 400 francs a month. Of course, more is possible with increased effort and good preparation. In general, however, this business idea is more suitable for earning extra money than for making a living from it.

What requirements are important for the successful implementation of the survey idea?

Interested parties do not need to make any major preparations in advance to participate in paid online surveys. Special qualifications are also not required in the simplest case.

The first step is to filter out the appropriate portal or portals for answering the relevant surveys. There are certainly differences in the payment systems, thematic focus and a few other areas. It is best to get a broad overview directly from the individual providers at the very beginning.

It is important to provide as much personal information as possible during the registration process. This does not only refer to data that is necessary for legal requirements and correct payment processing. As a rule, your own interests and experience must also be stated comprehensively and in detail.

This information usually forms the basis for being considered for surveys to which you can really make a useful contribution. This, in turn, is important for the recognition of performance and ultimate payment.

Online Shop classic

Online store as a digital business idea: Efficient sales opportunities, but often fierce competition

Setting up an online store is the digital business idea par excellence. There are numerous sales opportunities with two typical basic requirements:

1. In general, a web store either complements a stationary store and thus forms an additional sales channel.

2. Or it is used on its own or as a center of business activity, with all trade passing through it.

Both physical goods and services can be sold to customers in an online store. It is suitable for both B2C and B2B sales - depending on the company's focus.

What is the market like for online stores?

In fact, using the opportunities offered by online retail is now less of a nice-to-have and more of a must-have in many business areas.As the Internet becomes more and more integrated into everyday life, typical shopping behavior is also increasingly shifting to the online world.This applies to both the private and business environment.

While retailers and their offers used to take center stage, today the focus is increasingly shifting to customers and their wishes and needs. If you can't find what you're looking for in one place, you can quickly look elsewhere online.The opportunity to obtain meaningful advice on thousands of online platforms and then immediately purchase the relevant product on the web has led to the development of a completely new customer self-image that can only be adequately satisfied online. The business significance of web

stores is correspondingly high and the opportunities are correspondingly diverse.

Despite all the possible advantages, it should also be noted that there is now an almost unquantifiable number of online stores for every conceivable product. Surviving this competition is anything but easy and can only succeed with the right strategy.

How can you earn money with the online store idea?

Operators of online stores naturally earn money first and foremost through the sale of the products they offer. Other sources of income can also arise in the longer term. Advertising space in particular is a reliable earning option for well-visited multi-brand stores. Companies such as Amazon or eBay have also shown that clever e-commerce concepts can develop into much more - right up to gigantic ecosystems worth billions.

For both brick-and-mortar retailers and pure e-commerce companies entering the online business, a differentiated calculation of prices and costs is the be-all and end-all for financial success. A realistic pricing policy determines whether a company can operate profitably in the tough competition of e-commerce in the long term.

Quite a few online retailers are surprised when looking for a quote for the creation of an online store: the store system itself, the hosting costs and the individual development with sufficient visual features and usability functions can quickly mean costs in the five-digit range.

This high financial outlay is only worthwhile if a differentiated price calculation for the goods or services offered is a prerequisite. Ultimately, those who continuously review and develop their calculations will be able to deal correctly with recurring market-relevant price adjustments and continue to operate profitably.

What requirements are important for the successful implementation of the online store idea?

It is very important not to view the online store and the project in question as a construction kit with static processes. The store and its sales should be treated as part of e-commerce and a corresponding strategy. E-commerce is constantly evolving on several levels. Only those who optimally accept and implement this genesis in their project will be able to survive the often tough competition.

Above all, customer expectations should be met as comprehensively as possible. This applies to the product selection and prices as well as the brand presentation, design, usability and many other typical touchpoints. If a store is not fully convincing, it is very likely that potential customers will quickly turn to the (probably larger) competition.

In connection with the latter point, it is also essential to create unique selling points. Ideally, you should offer goods or services online that are not available anywhere else. This gives you the best chance of maximum success. Unfortunately, such unique business propositions are now relatively unlikely. There is almost nothing that cannot be bought online. Nevertheless, it can be worth entering the business if outstanding added value is provided in individual areas - from the product range to the shipping options.

Drop shipping

Drop shipping as a digital business idea: earning money online as a goods broker is relatively easy

Drop shipping is a special form of e-commerce. In the course of this, goods are practically brokered. Drop shippers generally enter into cooperation partnerships with suppliers and/or manufacturers of products and then sell these via their own online store, marketplaces or social media channels.

The highlight: the items on offer do not have to be purchased, stored and then shipped by the partners themselves, as is the case with conventional online retail. They remain in the partners' warehouses until actual purchases are made. They then send the goods directly to the end customer - without a detour via the drop shipper.

On a technical level, special drop-shipping software or an add-on that can be added to a well-known store system ensures an uncomplicated and fast process. When selling via one or more marketplaces, the processes are even simpler. This variant of online retail is therefore the simplest business idea in e-commerce in terms of the value chain.

What is the market like for drop shipping?

In fact, there are a great many drop shippers: a staggering 23% of all online purchases are already said to be made on the basis of drop shipping. This is suggested by various sources in statistics collections (including Shift4Shop). This of course means immense competition. Competition in e-commerce is generally fierce, which is why a sophisticated strategy is needed to survive - and not just in drop shipping.

Basically, the chances of success under this main premise are pretty good. Drop-shipping has a lot of potential, simply because online shopping continues to increase and people expect to be able to purchase more and more specialized products online.

The big advantage here is that the corresponding transactions can be processed with minimal effort. Once the products or the relevant contracts with the cooperation partners are in place, your own online store is filled and goods are offered that are really in demand, everything else practically runs by itself with the right system.

It should also be borne in mind that the most comprehensive product catalogs possible are in high demand among consumers today. Online stores that cover a wide range of needs (in a particular segment) are generally particularly popular. Drop shippers can meet this important market requirement themselves with comparatively little effort. After all, they only have to broker the numerous goods and not store and ship them themselves.

How can you earn money with the drop shipping idea?

Earnings from drop shipping (similar to conventional e-commerce) depend heavily on which products are sold, the prices at which they are sold and how high the other costs of the business are. Above all, the expenses for suppliers, the store system and marketing must be calculated.

In general, drop shippers have to reckon with significantly lower outlay than is required for traditional online trading. A drop shipping company can be set up with relatively small capital - the financial pressure is considerably lower. There is usually no need to contribute resources such as a warehouse or staff. Conversely, this means more potential for a large profit margin than would be possible for similarly priced products with a classic online store approach.

Nevertheless, it is important to know all the cost factors in the company and to include them proportionately in the calculation of each individual price.

What requirements are important for the successful implementation of the drop shipping idea?

A successful drop-shipping business naturally depends primarily on suitable products. To find suitable goods, drop shippers should invest some time in market research. At best, a niche can be found in which competition is relatively low.

In order to achieve noticeable success, competitors should also be closely examined. By analyzing the top competition, you can gain many useful insights into their working methods, pricing and marketing approaches. Such knowledge helps to make your own offering competitive and to diversify better.

On the one hand, reliable suppliers are the basic prerequisite for being able to operate drop shipping at all. On the other hand, it is only possible to generate long-term and secure sales with the right partners. Care should be taken to ensure that the quality of the products is right. The quality of deliveries and other service aspects must also be good. The goods should mainly be shipped quickly and arrive undamaged: Just as the respective target group expects.

Last but not least, drop shippers need one or more effective channels through which they can bring their offers to buyers. The classic choice here is the online store. In this context, the store system in the background must have the right options to allow drop shipping. Using a marketplace such as Amazon makes things a little easier. However, there are also considerable fees to be paid for using the platform.

Once all these requirements have been optimally considered, it is important to adequately promote your own e-commerce. A suitable marketing strategy is essential: from advertisements to content marketing, social media marketing and SEO through to influencer marketing, all options should be considered. Because, as I said, the competition is huge - and only those who position themselves ideally can survive.

PLATFORM

Marketplace platform as a digital business idea: earn money online with every third-party transaction

Today, marketplace platforms can be found in many business areas and for a wide variety of goods and services. Corresponding offerings give numerous sellers - retailers as well as manufacturers - the opportunity to sell their products within an (ideally) established e-commerce solution.

Participants create an account and can then sell their articles to their customers quickly and easily using standardized and generally very simple tools or processes.

The operator itself does not necessarily have to use its marketplace to sell its own product range. He earns primarily through the commission he collects from his partners for each of their transactions. There are also other sources of income.

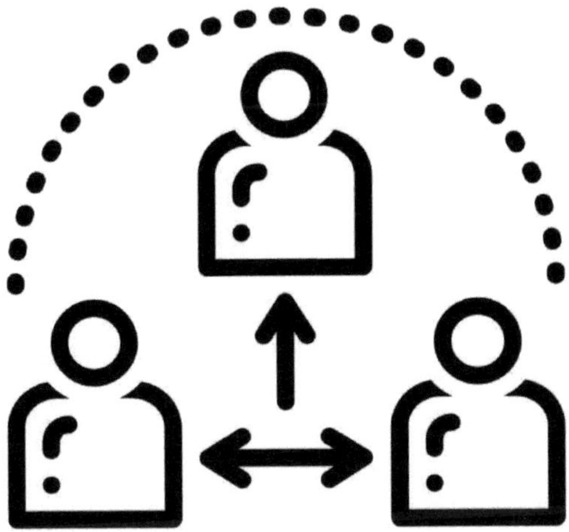

What is the market for marketplace platforms like?

Online retail is still booming. It can therefore be worth investing in a corresponding business or becoming an e-commercer yourself. The option of setting up your own marketplace platform is particularly attractive because such offers - if they are well made - are generally well received by online shoppers.

A key reason for this is that physical goods in particular, but also services, can be sold comparatively cheaply on such a platform. This is because retailers or manufacturers only have a relatively small outlay when selling there. They do have to pay commission to the operator for every transaction concluded. However, these costs are relatively low compared to setting up and maintaining an online store in the long term.

In addition, potential buyers often find particularly large product ranges in a specific segment or across product types on marketplace platforms. This is mainly because many retailers and producers choose relatively simple marketplace sales. The extensive selection is in turn extremely attractive for end consumers, as they can ideally get everything they are looking for from a single source and do not have to spend a lot of time researching.

The use of the marketplace idea therefore has enormous potential. However, it should not be concealed that a great deal of effort is required to be successful with such a platform.

How can you earn money with the marketplace platform idea?

A marketplace platform offers various opportunities to earn money:

1. **Commission fees:** First of all, there is the typical commission income. Every retailer or manufacturer who wants to sell their products on a marketplace must pay a certain percentage of their earnings or (often above a certain purchase value) a fixed amount to the platform operator. Normally, this is charged per transaction.
2. **Monthly basic fees:** The second possible source of income is a monthly basic fee that the partners registered on the platform pay to the operator. Such fees are absolutely legitimate due to the considerable hosting and maintenance costs associated with maintaining the system.
3. **Advertising spaces:** There is generally a lot of traffic on an established marketplace platform. This in turn makes the offer extremely interesting for advertisers. The greater the volume of visitors, the more money the operator can charge for prominent advertising space - i.e. banners, video clips, blog posts, etc. - charge.
4. **Special services:** There are many opportunities to offer partners of a marketplace platform additional services and earn money with them. For example, brands can be promoted within special newsletter sections for a fee, products can be highlighted in the search ranking with the help of ads or there are special display functions for brand presentation for an additional charge.

What requirements are important for the successful implementation of the marketplace platform idea?

The major challenge with the platform idea is to publicize the marketplace and establish it in such a way that as many retailers or producers as possible as well as numerous buyers find their way there. At the very base, it is necessary to provide both sides - i.e. potential partners and potential customers - with an optimal user experience.

The platform must provide sellers with simple but powerful features to present their products in the perfect light. End customers, on the other hand, want to find exactly what they are looking for quickly and easily. Ideally, expectations are met at all levels and exceeded at critical points. For example, if brands have the opportunity to highlight their USPs individually or consumers can use particularly simple search inputs (e.g. voice search), this is likely to be very well received.

Another key criterion for the success of the marketplace approach is the clever calculation of the commission for sales, the monthly basic fee, the prices for advertising and the expenses for any additional services. All these costs should support your own business and generate a profit, but should also be below the expenses that the target retailer group would have to invest for sales in their own online store.

AFFILIATES

Affiliates as a digital business idea: earn money through the clicks of others

Affiliates are partners of companies (even literally translated) who advertise their goods or services. Corresponding companies thus engage in affiliate marketing. This means that they have part of the customer acquisition and retention for their products carried out by the aforementioned partners or affiliates.

This promotion or marketing by third parties takes place on specific websites. Typical media are blogs, e-commerce sites, but also social media such as Facebook, Twitter or YouTube. Affiliates provide companies with space for banners, text ads, clips or other online advertising media. The promotions are provided with links to individual offers from the partner companies or to entire brands.

For example, if interested parties click on a banner showing a popular razor from a partner company, they are taken directly to this product. The affiliate receives a commission for the referral if the potential customer actually becomes a buyer, in this case by purchasing the razor. In addition to this model, there are other monetization approaches.

However, good and successful affiliates offer much more than just advertising space (otherwise they would effectively just be ad publishers). They actually market their partners' offers and engage in clever, very subtle marketing to convince buyers to take a closer look at the promoted articles or brands.

What is the market like for affiliates?

The main advantage of affiliate marketing for companies is that they can bring their goods or services to their target group very precisely and with a wide reach via corresponding partners at a relatively low financial outlay. This works precisely when the affiliates operate online presences that operate in the same business environment as the companies themselves and also regularly receive a large number of visitors.

It is primarily for these reasons that there are so many companies using affiliate marketing today, which in turn means huge potential for affiliates. Statista analyses suggest that the current affiliate marketing turnover in German-speaking countries alone is well over 10 billion euros per year. The figures have been rising for years.

How can you earn money with the affiliate idea?

Affiliates' income is always based on a commission model. This can take various forms.

- **Pay-per-sale:** In the most widespread variant, a percentage of the sales price of the linked product is paid. This means that affiliates are only paid when sales are made.
- **Pay-per-lead:** With this billing option, payment depends on whether the affiliate's activities result in contacts between potential customers and companies.
- **Lifetime commission:** This model can be very lucrative, but is also rare. Affiliates receive commissions again and again after a click (and usually after a resulting deal) if referred customers generate sales for the partner companies.
- **Pay-per-click:** Here, affiliates aim to force clicks from potential buyers. Each time a link is clicked, they collect a predetermined amount. This does not have to be completed.
- **Pay-per-view:** This monetization approach does not even require clicks. The decisive factor for payment is the pure display of advertising material from the partner companies.

But how do affiliates find the right partner companies? This is actually relatively easy today: the numerous affiliate portals available on the Internet are particularly suitable for getting started. A wide variety of companies cavort on these and offer their partner programs.

After registration, a short application is sometimes required for participation in certain programs. In this way, the companies check whether the affiliates match their own services. After acceptance, you can get started.

What requirements are important for the successful implementation of the affiliate idea?

If you want to become a successful affiliate, you should have sufficient expertise in online marketing and ideally also in web design. It is fundamentally important for companies that their products reach and convince the right target group on their partners' websites, are presented in the best possible way and are easy to find. They want to benefit as fully as possible from the core benefits of affiliate marketing.

Tools for designing user-friendly online channels, content marketing and SEO are key tools for affiliates to create ideal conditions. If these and other tools are optimally harmonized, the result is high traffic and thus all the more generous income. The more visitors from a relevant target group an affiliate has on its website, the more valuable it is for partner companies and the greater its earning potential.

News platform

News platform as a digital business idea: earn money through special interest content, advertising, etc.

People want to be informed and stay informed. Particularly in this day and age, when the internet with its huge variety of content is always and everywhere available via smartphones, the desire of many to always be promptly up to date is increasing. As a result, there are numerous large and small news platforms that enable interested parties to access exactly the news that corresponds to their interests.

In certain cases, users are quite prepared to pay for the services of these sites. In addition to direct payment, there are also other ways to generate revenue with or via news portals.

Setting up a web presence with news, feeds, newsletters and everything that typical users of such platforms expect is even relatively easy with the right tools. The greater difficulty usually lies in regularly filling it with the perfect content, attracting readers, convincing them across the board and gaining a good reputation in the long term.

What is the market like for news platforms?

News platforms and news sites are very popular among the population. More and more people prefer to use the internet to obtain information on all kinds of issues relating to their everyday lives - whether it's advice on buying a new electric car or help with operating their fully automatic coffee machine. News from society, politics, culture, technology, hobbies, etc. are no longer mainly obtained from daily newspapers and magazines. The Internet is also the first choice in these areas.

In some cases, this results in enormous visitor numbers: For example, according to Statista, **Bild.de is one of the largest news platforms in Europe with more than 500 million visits per month. Of course, it is not easy to reach this level of traffic. The daily newspaper has been a fixture in the German-speaking world for decades. But even smaller portals and special interest sites in technology, sport, cooking, etc. can quickly have several**

hundred thousand or even millions of regular users. This is shown by various national and international studies on the subject - including those conducted by the Informationsgemeinschaft zur Feststellung der Verbreitung von Werbeträgern e.V. (IVW).

Wherever there are many interested parties and visitors online, there are always good opportunities to earn money. We have already seen this at one point or another in the last few chapters. Consequently, a news platform has great financial potential.

How can you earn money with the news platform idea?

A news platform offers various opportunities to earn money. If you are the operator of such a portal, you can sell the news service itself or the news on it. Many regional and national daily newspapers follow such an approach in their offerings: If you want to read the whole article, you need a subscription.

Competing successfully with large and established news providers such as Bild.de or smaller platforms that have been around for a long time is, of course, anything but easy. However, if you have managed to build up a certain and growing circle of regular users, you can expect not only many subscribers, but also additional income.

Many news platforms - de facto even those that are basically free to use - generate revenue by selling advertising space: The more users there are, the greater the revenue generally is. The advertising is ultimately paid for via one of numerous commission models. The contracts or remuneration are either negotiated individually or, if you join a larger network, are set up with predefined conditions.

The most common alternative to setting up a news platform is to work as an author for a news portal. Payment is then normally made on a word and/or commission basis. Specialized services such as the United States Press Agency even offer authors the opportunity to open their own portals or personal departments, manage them independently and thus earn an income. This can also provide helpful experience for the eventual creation of your own platform.

What requirements are important for the successful implementation of the news platform idea?

As mentioned above, it is quite a challenge to set up a news portal yourself and be successful with it. The creation itself is no problem for digitally savvy founders using standard web design construction kits. However, creating the conditions for actually earning money with the platform is much more difficult.

Users or readers and the traffic they generate are an important key to success. It is important to convince as many people as possible - above all - with the content offered. This includes not only addressing exactly the topics that the readership wants, but also staying on the ball and regularly posting news - ideally ahead of the competition.

Achieving this is extremely difficult in general information areas relating to society, politics and tabloids, especially for newcomers. Enormous amounts of information have to be sifted through and promptly implemented in order to operate competitively on the market. Special interest content on technology, hobbies, lifestyle etc. is more suitable here.

Suitable authors can be found via freelancer portals such as Fiverr or Textbroker. You can also get help with important marketing and SEO measures at these addresses.

Blogger

Bloggers as a digital business idea: generating income by publishing expert knowledge

Originally, the blog was intended as a kind of digital diary through which the public could participate in the life of the blogger. Initially, such websites were called web logs ("web logbook"), but this soon changed in everyday language to the term we use today. The basic principle has always remained the same:

Individual authors or several writers regularly publish articles in a blog on a specific topic area that is of interest to a larger target group. Readers are given the opportunity to comment on what has been written.

Blogging was quickly adopted by companies to disseminate information - from developments in the company to new products and supporting content for (potential) customers. In the latter context in particular, blogs have become hugely relevant over the past ten years:

People are increasingly looking for information online that really helps them to solve a problem or meet a need. Blogs are an ideal medium for communicating such content because they are flexible, versatile and easy to update.

More and more sole traders and freelancers are also taking advantage of this situation. They blog professionally and attract thousands of people to their blogs every month by sharing their expert knowledge. This traffic is extremely interesting for companies if they operate in the same business context as a successful blogger. This is because they can reach a large number of people from their own customer base. This in turn means great earning potential for the blog operator. The rule is: the more visitors, the more you can earn.

What is the market like for bloggers?

High-quality, genuinely helpful content is in demand: studies by Demand Gen Report, Demand Metrics and other research institutions suggest that over 50 percent of consumers now view several pieces of related online content before making a purchase to help them make their buying decision.

Furthermore, around 70 percent prefer to get the facts they need from independent blogs rather than corporate sites.

The importance of strong, relevant content is therefore considerable for companies. According to a collection of statistics from HubSpot, blogging is one of the most important tools in the content marketing strategy of 53% of marketers.

The great popularity of external company blogs among consumers is extremely interesting for freelance bloggers: Blog articles that appear outside a company network and are also not written by company employees offer outstanding potential for persuasion. They are written by bloggers who are experts in their industry and/or have actually bought and tested the products in question. This makes the views, opinions and perspectives conveyed absolutely authentic.

Customers are much less likely to expect marketing strategies behind external blog content than if the same content had appeared on a company website. It is precisely such real (or seemingly real) evaluations from experts outside of companies that relatively often provide today's prospective customers with the final impulse that turns them into buyers. Various surveys suggest that more than 60 percent are more likely to buy a product if it is recommended by independent experts.

These figures and correlations leave no doubt that bloggers can be extremely valuable for brands in all business areas.

How can you earn money with the blogger idea?

There are many ways to earn money as a blogger. The following ways are particularly common.

- **Pay-per-click advertising:** With this type of blog monetization, ad spaces on the website are initially made available for advertisements. After registering with a service for pay-per-click promotions such as Google AdSense, the service places ads in the designated locations. A commission is paid for each click.

- **Rent advertising space directly:** As an alternative or in addition to pay-per-click advertising, there is the opportunity to rent advertising space directly to partner companies, i.e. without an intermediary service. This involves more effort, but you can also earn more, as the contracts and remuneration can be negotiated individually.
- **Affiliate links:** Affiliate links work in a similar way to pay-per-click advertising. However, the blogger integrates the ads or text links themselves.
- **Sponsored posts:** Sponsored posts are blog posts that focus specifically on individual products or brands. The companies concerned pay for a prominent presentation of their services on high-traffic blogs.
- **Guest posts:** Anyone who has achieved a certain expert status as a blogger is also of interest to other blog operators in the same subject area. Guest posts by such experts attract many readers. Renowned guest writers can be well paid for this additional traffic potential.
- **Paid content:** Blogs and ultimately bloggers thrive on high-quality content. Web users are prepared to pay money for content with outstanding added value, such as white papers, test reports or guides.

What requirements are important for the successful implementation of the blogger idea?

If you want to earn money as a blogger, you first need a blog, of course. This can be easily created with one of the many available blog providers or website builders, even by non-professionals.

After that, however, it becomes more difficult: The two elementary components for successful blogging are:

1. The regular publication of highly valuable content.

2. Obtaining expert status in your own subject area.

Only under these conditions can sufficient traffic be generated for bloggers to benefit from all the monetization opportunities listed above.

In order to achieve this, specialist knowledge and creativity are essential skills on a textual level. In terms of technology and strategy, networking, SEO and content marketing should be among the blogger's strengths.

Backlink Seller

Backlink seller as a digital business idea: earn money by selling links

Website operators - be they bloggers, e-commerce companies, influencers or comparison portal providers - can earn money from the links that lead from their websites to other sites. So-called backlinks are important ranking factors.

The principle is relatively simple: sellers (publishers) rent out space for backlinks in their content. The links lead to precisely matched pages of corresponding buyers (advertisers). They are generally positioned in texts that serve the same thematic focus as the target pages or are at least close to it. At best, a logical connection between the two pages becomes clear via the links and the corresponding anchor texts. Publishers generally receive a fixed amount per month for the link space.

Such links are seen by Google as recommendations. If a page and the associated website are linked to many pages on the same topic that are of good quality, the search engine leader tends to give a better ranking. The conclusion that Google draws here is: "If a page is positively mentioned (linked) by numerous other pages, it must provide outstanding added value in its subject area, which means that it should be positioned at the top for the relevant search queries."

What is the market like for backlink sellers?

Backlinks are still one of Google's top three most important ranking factors. Such links provide the search engine with a lot of orientation on the web, establish important connections for its evaluations and thus assign them a correspondingly high relevance for the establishment of its rankings.

For these reasons, backlinks and link building always have a firm place in well thought-out and comprehensive SEO strategies.

Especially in competitive markets, backlinks often make the difference. As a result, large, financially strong companies in particular are very keen to obtain many high-quality links and dig deep into their pockets to do so. However, smaller companies or those with less competition are also increasingly recognizing their opportunities. This is because they can often extend their lead over their competitors on Google with backlinks.

All this means a lot of potential for backlink sellers.

How can you earn money with the backlink seller idea?

The value of backlinks is usually determined on the basis of various factors. These include usability, the added value of the content, the scope of the content, the technical implementation, the guarantee of uniqueness, the last update date, the traffic and the authority with Google.

Good agencies pay publishers between 20 and several thousand euros per month for suitable link positions. With automated services, the remuneration is usually somewhat lower, but backlink sales are all the easier.

This brings us to the most common options for backlink sellers: there are basically three options open to interested parties.

1. **Automated backlink brokerage service:** There are various backlink services on the web through which companies can buy links and website operators can sell suitable link spaces. These services are largely automated. As a seller, you use code to establish a connection between the service and your own website, define the pages on which links to other pages may appear, wait for implementation and finally for the monthly payment.

2. **Backlink agency:** Working with a backlink agency is usually much more personal. You have a contact person and get the chance to negotiate remuneration on a more individual basis.

3. **Direct cooperation:** Direct cooperation and personalized remuneration offer the most freedom and the greatest earning potential. However, the workload is also highest here.

What requirements are important for the successful implementation of the backlink seller idea?

At the very base, prospective backlink sellers naturally need one or more websites on which they can offer links. In order to achieve the highest possible sales prices, these blogs, online stores, advice portals etc. should score highly in all relevant review categories of potential partners.

This means that backlink sellers ideally ensure optimal usability, great added value in terms of content, reasonable scope, up-to-date technical implementation, unique content, topicality, reliable traffic and a high authority with Google.

This requires some work and, not least, sound knowledge of web design, content marketing, SEO and online marketing in general. Interested parties are also well advised to find out exactly what the rules of link building are and to take them into account when selling backlinks. There are some dangers lurking here.

Above all, it is important to minimize the risks associated with selling links and to keep the quality of your own web presence high. The buying and selling of backlinks is not welcomed by Google.

- To avoid being penalized by the search engine, it is better to offer only a small number of link positions. It is better to focus on class rather than quantity. Accordingly, it is better to provide fewer positions, but on pages of particularly high quality.
- It is also advisable to check the link partners carefully and, if necessary, reject requests. This is because contextually inappropriate links, which may also come from pages of a lower quality, can have a negative impact on your own pages.

The interrelationships are complex, which is why it is extremely important to have a good overview of the subject matter.

Freelancer

Freelancer as a digital business idea: earning money as a freelancer through skill and expertise

The English term "freelancer" translates as "free employee". Freelancers are self-employed people who often provide their labor not only to a single company in a typical employment relationship, but also provide services for several companies. They run their own business in which they offer their creativity, expertise and/or special skills to companies.

The conditions of the work - and above all the payment - can be set out in a contract. However, there is often a partnership based on trust, which may only be framed by very important legal regulations, such as a confidentiality agreement.

Freelancers are not bound by instructions. They should act in the interests of the companies and contacts with whom they work. In principle, however, they can "do what they want": this means above all that such workers plan the work they are assigned independently and, if necessary, have the option of rejecting it. They sometimes carry out their tasks on the premises of their clients. Most of the time, however, they carry out their work in their own offices or from home.

The latter freedoms in particular make working as a freelancer extremely attractive - especially for well-trained and therefore sought-after specialists.

What is the market like for freelancers?

Freelancers are in high demand in many industries. The fact that quite a few companies only need certain specialists for temporary projects or need to call on them regularly, but not on a daily basis, makes the option of employing freelancers extremely attractive.

In fact, freelancers can often offer companies a particularly high level of qualification and therefore ultimately outstanding results. Experienced freelancers in particular have seen a lot in the course of their career and draw on a broad knowledge of their business area. They are also less business-blind and more able to think outside the box than in-house employees in the same specialist area. They provide new ideas and encourage different ways of thinking. Many managers are fully aware of this, which is why they are happy to work with freelancers.

Freelancers are also extremely flexible. Especially in creative fields, they often work faster and with more customization options than agencies. They are available for projects at short notice, promptly take on stand-ins and/or schedule weekend to-dos in an emergency. In general, good freelancers who have been self-employed for several years are characterized by an outstanding willingness to work and the utmost discipline. Otherwise they would not have been able to maintain their business for so long. It goes without saying that these qualities are well received by many companies.

Last but not least, freelancers are often relatively inexpensive. They have no fixed personnel costs and very little administrative work. If a freelancer falls ill, they do not have to be paid. Freelancers pay their health, pension and long-term care insurance entirely out of their own pocket. When working independently from home, companies do not even have to calculate the costs of premises or technology.

These arguments clearly speak in favor of working with freelancers, which companies like to make frequent use of. This means a lot of potential for the freelancer's business idea.

How can you earn money with the freelancer idea?

Freelancers are paid per hour according to the amount of work, specialist knowledge and experience. Beginners or newcomers to the profession in particular are well advised not to put all their eggs in one basket straight away and to start out as a freelancer on a part-time basis. Before you can earn your own living, you first have to build up a certain reputation in your sector.

As explained above, freelancers are generally in high demand in many business contexts. There are particularly good opportunities in creative fields and software development. But self-employed accountants, engineers and healthcare professionals are also regularly in demand.

Consultants or advisors are generally the highest earners. With a good reputation, they often earn 200 or 300 francs an hour. Marketing experts are similarly well paid.

What requirements are important for the successful implementation of the freelancer idea?

At a very basic level, freelancers must have specific skills that they can provide to companies as freelancers. These skills should also be in high demand. The expertise and the associated range of services must then be made known to the widest possible range of potential employers or clients.

A sufficient web presence, i.e. a website and social media channels, is essential for this. There are also special platforms for freelancers, such as Freelancer-Schweiz.ch or Fiverr, where self-employed people can present themselves and interested companies can search specifically for suitable specialists. Registration on these platforms is quick and easy and provides very useful coverage.

To get off to a good start as a freelancer and be successful in the long term, you also need enormous discipline, motivation, a lot of willingness to work independently, entrepreneurial understanding, organizational talent and the best communication, cooperation and networking skills.

YOUTUBER

YouTubers as a digital business idea: generating revenue through outstanding video added value

YouTuber is actually a widely recognized profession today. Younger people in particular know that it is possible to earn money through activities on the popular video platform. For many, being a YouTuber is even a dream job that sounds easy to get into.

However, it takes a lot more than some people think to be successful in this field. Of course, YouTubers start by creating videos and making them accessible to the general public. With more than 2.5 billion users per month worldwide, the video service offers ideal conditions for this.

However, in order for a sufficient number of people to become aware of your channel, subscribe to it and regularly watch the corresponding posts, it is important to provide outstanding added value in terms of information, expertise and/or entertainment. It should be borne in mind that it is only possible to earn money with a YouTube channel if it has at least 1,000 subscribers.

The display options are almost endless, but unfortunately the competition is also huge.

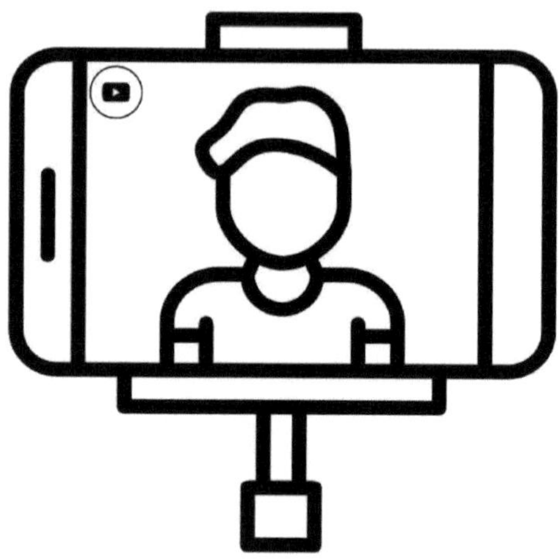

What is the market like for YouTubers?

YouTube is not only the most widely used video platform in the world today, but also the second-largest search engine after Google. Various studies suggest that in German-speaking countries alone, well over 80 percent of people regularly watch YouTube content. Many of them are now specifically looking there for help with everyday questions or problems, as is also the case with Google's search engine.

The clear advantage that YouTube has over a classic search engine in the latter context lies in the medium of video. With the help of short or longer films, facts - even complex relationships - can be presented and explained in a very catchy way if implemented well. In addition, videos are easy and relatively quick for users to record. Obtaining information is generally less complicated with moving images than with the same content in text form, for example.

This in turn is a determining factor in the fact that video is extremely popular with internet users today in all kinds of application contexts and is therefore widely used. People have less and less time and leisure to engage with content, but still want helpful, detailed and entertaining added value. Videos can meet these requirements.

On the other hand, more and more companies want to benefit from the great interest in videos and YouTube. They have long since recognized the huge reach of the channel and are promoting their products and brands there with immense success. The best YouTube channels can get a good slice of this pie if they enter into partnerships with such companies.

All in all, these conditions mean enormous potential for YouTubers.

How can you earn money with the YouTuber idea?

YouTubers generally earn money through advertising that is broadcast in their videos. There are different options available. The following options are particularly typical and can be implemented even by beginners.

- **Ads:** Ads are still and will probably continue to be the primary way for YouTubers to earn money. YouTube is part of the Google AdSense advertising network. This means that suitable promotions can be automatically inserted within videos and revenue can be generated through user clicks on these. This makes monetization particularly easy for YouTubers.

- **Affiliate links:** YouTubers can also independently place affiliate links in their content. Income is usually generated when YouTube users click on such a link and buy a product behind it. Sometimes it is even enough for them to simply follow a link - depending on the agreement.

- **Individual advertising partnerships:** Another very common source of income are individual partnerships with companies that integrate advertising into YouTubers' content. Such promotions are then placed directly in the videos and not interposed as with AdSense. This variant is increasingly preferred by companies, as the corresponding clips cannot be switched off by adblockers.

In addition to these monetization opportunities, YouTubers - especially established ones - have a number of other options: for example, channel memberships, merchandising articles or (especially for international musicians) concert tickets can also be sold via the video platform.

What requirements are important for the successful implementation of the YouTuber idea?

First of all, to be successful as a YouTuber, you should cover a subject area that is of interest to as many people as possible. Ideally, you should serve a popular niche and/or focus on content with added value that no one else offers.

Skills in video editing and design must be available or acquired. In addition, it is important for typical YouTubers to be able to present themselves positively and verbally convey knowledge or entertainment to others. The right tone of voice, a suitable speaking speed, optimal auditory and content comprehensibility and much more is crucial for whether videos are accepted by a broad mass of people or not.

For it to be possible to earn money on YouTube at all, four basic requirements must be met:

1. Your own channel must comply with YouTube's guidelines and must not have a warning.
2. There are at least 1,000 subscribers and the clips have a playback time of 4,000 hours over the last 12 months.
3. The terms of use of the YouTube partner program must be accepted.
4. An account should be created with Google AdSense and linked to the YouTube channel.

SOCIAL MEDIA INFLUENCER

Social media influencers as a digital business idea: generating income as opinion leaders for companies

Social media influencers are people who have a strong presence on Instagram, YouTube, X and the like. This primarily means that they regularly post content that is helpful or simply entertaining in some way and therefore many people follow them. Through their posts, which have a correspondingly large reach, they inform, influence and form opinions among their followers.

The content usually covers a specific subject area in which the influencer in question positions themselves as an expert or trustworthy authority. This is determined by various factors, such as education or professional background, practical experience and sometimes "just" a heightened and externalized interest. No matter how an influencer profiles themselves as an expert in their field, at best they come across as genuine, independent, serious, credible and convincing. This is precisely why they have so many followers.

This in turn is very interesting for companies that do business in the same subject area as a particular influencer. The latter can earn money by promoting the products, procedures and/or views of such companies to the people who follow them.

What is the market like for social media influencers?

Social media influencers usually act as independent personalities. If they do their job well, they have a high profile and reach a large number of people. Their appearance and the use of social networks for their publications make them appear comparatively approachable.

The social web generally has a predominantly private atmosphere. In addition to entertainment and communication between acquaintances, business, scientific, political, technical or other information with high added value can be communicated in a very informal way. Together with the often direct interaction between influencers and their followers via likes, comments and possibly even chats, this allows for truly personal contact.

This is precisely what makes good social media influencers so credible and why so many companies use them today. Companies are given the opportunity to communicate their products, procedures or opinions very precisely, individually and intimately to their respective target group or the followers of the influencer in question. The opinion leaders' fans pick up on these messages and act on them relatively frequently.

In terms of the persuasive power of influencers for purchases, partnerships or other business, German-speaking countries are still lagging behind internationally. Nevertheless, the figures are rising continuously and more and more companies are spending a lot of money on such promotions.

- According to Statista, twelve percent of young Swiss people (aged 13 to 30) count influencers among their top sources for purchasing decisions.
- The economic policy magazine "Die Volkswirtschaft" has analyzed data according to which the market share of influencer marketing in Switzerland is expected to reach almost CHF 200 million by 2027.

This all means enormous potential for companies and people who want to earn money as influencers.

How can you earn money with the social media influencer idea?

Anyone who wants to earn money as a social media influencer usually does so through partnerships with various companies. Depending on the level of awareness or number of followers, negotiating skills and individual agreements, the amount of the fee varies.

Basically, it is always about promoting products, procedures or opinions of the partner companies. The income is usually calculated per post in which a corresponding promotion takes place.

The more people follow a social media influencer, the more they can charge for a post. It is difficult to say in general terms how much this will ultimately amount to. However, there are certain guidelines for each type of influencer.

- **Micro-influencers:** Such influencers have around 500 to 10,000 followers (definition values vary). This is not a large number in comparison, but the corresponding contacts tend to be particularly loyal. This is why such opinion leaders can earn 500 to 1,000 francs per post in certain business areas.
- **Conventional influencers:** The normal influencer has 100,000+ followers. This potential reach is of course extremely attractive for companies. That's why 5,000 Swiss francs per post is absolutely possible here. If it goes well over 100,000 or even a million fans, the earnings margin is even higher.

What requirements are important for the successful implementation of the social media influencer idea?

First of all, social media influencers must have certain qualities that are of interest to others. This can be outstanding expertise in a certain area, a high entertainment value, but also "just" good looks.

They should also know how social networks and the types of content they provide work, what makes their users tick and how they can best reach their target group. They must have the best skills for (product) presentation and self-presentation in personal appearance as well as image and sound technology.

Followers are their greatest asset. The more people follow a social media influencer, the greater their earning potential. Opinion leaders should therefore always maintain contact with their fans, interact with them personally and respond appropriately to their input and comments. Maintaining authenticity, credibility and independence is extremely important in this context.

VIRTUAL ASSISTANCE

Virtual assistance as a digital business idea: perform and earn typical business assistance tasks from home

Companies usually have numerous tasks that are difficult for the managers themselves or their employees to take on. However, hiring an on-site assistant is often not worthwhile. The solution: virtual assistance or a virtual assistant. Such staff support managing directors, consultants or teams in larger, but above all smaller companies as external service providers. They work on account and organize their assignments independently.

This help can relate to a wide variety of specialist areas or tasks - depending on the work that needs to be done in the respective company. In most cases, these are recurring and time-consuming tasks. The aim of outsourcing is generally to gain more time for the core business. For companies, the possibility of outsourcing means great flexibility. For the virtual assistants, it offers a lot of variety.

What is the market like for virtual assistance?

Companies benefit from many advantages by using the services of a virtual assistant: Smaller companies in particular often cannot or do not want to afford to hire a special employee for important but perhaps not regularly performed accounting work, website maintenance or organizing appointments. A virtual assistant is often the perfect alternative here.

Such a service provider works independently and is paid exactly according to the workload. A company can choose to use their manpower on a daily basis, once a week or even just by the hour every few months. Virtual assistants are generally very flexible, which also gives potential clients a great deal of flexibility.

As a result, companies that work with virtual assistants generally get highly trained experts. As a rule, such freelancers are genuine specialists who offer their skills on their own after a career as an employee. Professionals in project management, content creation, SEO tasks or even experienced secretaries are in high demand and are therefore often booked.

The costs are fairly low compared to an employment contract. The mere fact that the rates are based on orders is often financially attractive for companies. In addition, they do not have to calculate expenses for office space or equipment, as a virtual assistant usually works within their own four walls and with personal equipment.

These are all good reasons why more and more managers in companies are relying on the services of a virtual assistant. This business idea therefore has great potential.

How can you earn money with virtual assistance?

A virtual assistant generally works independently and on a fee basis. How much they can earn depends primarily on the conditions of the job in question. Of course, factors such as training, experience and reputation also play an important role.

For example, a virtual assistant who has been employed as a project coordinator for years may be able to earn more than someone with less experience simply because of their professional routine. It is indeed possible to become self-employed as a virtual assistant without formal training or previous employment - but then you generally have to start low when it comes to earnings.

Under these basic conditions, there are numerous areas of work for a virtual assistant:

- General office or secretarial work
- Research work
- Data maintenance and preparation
- Creation of presentations

- Planning for appointments, events and trips
- Accounting, tax etc.
- Copywriting and PR
- Preparation of translations
- Website or online store maintenance
- Social media activities
- Graphic design or image editing

What requirements are important for the successful implementation of the virtual assistant idea?

A virtual assistant should be able to use a PC or notebook and typical office programs. A certain affinity for the Internet is also an advantage, as communication and ultimately many tasks are carried out online.

In order to be able to successfully sell professional services as a virtual assistant, you should also have proof of training (ideally in line with the intended activities) and a certain amount of professional experience. Neither of these is a must, but they increase the chances of your services being used by many clients, as well as your earning potential.

In most cases, virtual assistants work with several companies and therefore have to juggle various tasks and sometimes also numerous customers. In order to maintain an overview and always deliver the best results, an above-average level of self-organization, multitasking ability and motivation is essential. Openness to new ideas and enthusiasm are also important qualities - not least because you often have to take on tasks that clients may not like.

A self-confident appearance helps to convince potential customers. Acquisition is best done via social business networks, such as LinkedIn, or special freelancer platforms, i.e. Fiverr and the like. If you can communicate and network skillfully, are well trained and aware of your strengths, you will quickly find interested parties here.

Website & App Tester

Website and app testers as a digital business idea: earn money by testing and evaluating online applications

Website and app testers initially do exactly what the term suggests: They put relevant applications through their paces. This type of work falls into the broad area of crowd testing, which generally involves testing software, websites, apps or, in particular, computer games by large groups of test subjects.

The core task of such people is to click through a website or app, try out as many functions as possible and then report back. Sometimes only certain features need to be checked, such as a newly introduced online tool on a company website or the checkout process in an online store.

Website and app testers are briefed precisely in this context and should (in the simplest case) record exactly what they like in relation to the specifications, in which segments there may have been difficulties and where something may not have worked at all. The result is remunerated with a certain fee.

What is the market like for website and app testers?

(Potential) customers have long been using the internet and associated applications such as websites, forums, social media or apps to obtain all kinds of information. On the one hand, this relates to assistance with everyday questions or direct digital support (usually via apps) - for example, when creating shopping lists, planning sports activities, etc. On the other hand, advice on planned purchases and acquisitions is now also provided via such channels in many cases.

"Online" is therefore becoming increasingly important for companies: websites and apps not only have to be available these days, they also have to work perfectly anywhere, on all devices and with all software combinations. Only then are the associated companies truly competitive. Bugs or deficits in usability should not occur under any circumstances. Of course, these and similar errors are largely eliminated during development. However, whether everything runs perfectly can only be determined in a real user environment or with real users of the respective target group.

In this context, it is important to note that as websites or apps become increasingly mature, their functionalities also become more complex and extensive. This means that there are countless ways and possibilities in which significant negative effects can occur. This in turn makes it essential to obtain not only precise evaluations, but also evaluations from as many test subjects as possible.

This means that there is a great need for website and app testers, which in turn means a lot of potential for interested parties.

How can you earn money with the website and app tester idea?

Basically, those interested have two options for becoming a website or app tester and earning money with it:

1. You register with a crowdtesting platform such as testbirds.de, ap plause.com or rapidusertests.com and have orders placed through them.
2. Or they get in touch directly with companies or special digital agencies that regularly produce and test corresponding applications.

Payment is generally made on a fee basis - regardless of whether you cooperate with a platform or directly with specific partner companies.

There is a clear task for each individual test: for example, the search for spelling mistakes, the detection of functional deficits or the consideration of the overall user-friendliness or usability. In any case, the result must ultimately be documented clearly, comprehensibly and in accordance with the requirements.

The exact cost of all this depends on the level of detail of the task in all areas, i.e. auditing and reporting. The usual range per run is between around CHF 15 and CHF 100.

What requirements are important for the successful implementation of the website and app tester idea?

Especially for those who test websites or apps via a crowdtesting platform, it is not always immediately obvious that this is a self-employed activity. Earnings may have to be taxed and registration with the tax office is usually required.

If the associated requirements are met, it doesn't take much more to earn money as a website and app tester. Basically, you should have a certain affinity for online applications and you must belong to the target group of the company placing the order for some analyses. However, special training is not usually required.

"Mostly" because tests can sometimes also relate to more specific issues. For example, there are certainly offers that involve looking at SEO properties or analyzing individual design features from a professional point of view. Here, experts or at least people with basic experience always have a better chance of being brought on board and then earn more.

Product tester

Product testers as a digital business idea: generate income by testing food, electronics, lifestyle products and more

As a rule, product testers are tasked with testing and evaluating physical goods in a wide range of categories before they are officially launched on the market. The items to be tested are provided free of charge by the manufacturers. These are usually food, electronics or lifestyle products.

This business idea is digital because interested parties can register on various online portals for the placement of corresponding work. The organization is then largely handled by these intermediaries. The level of payment is also regulated here. If the job is done single-handedly, i.e. without an intermediary platform, the test results are often published on the Internet, which also provides a digital basis.

Of course, the check is not carried out randomly: providers generally set certain requirements for this, which are set out in a detailed briefing. Typical factors include the specification of specific features that must be scrutinized and the evaluation period or deadline for submitting the test results.

The experiences should always be honest and authentic. The goods are generally assessed in terms of functionality, handling, design, taste, smell, etc. -

depending on the product group. The companies want to find out whether the intention of their new developments is really being received as planned by the users or buyers. The final evaluation is carried out internally - and it is even possible that the testers' verdicts (if they are too negative) may result in the publication being canceled.

Sometimes items that are already on the market are also checked. This is often done because the manufacturer wants to generate ratings and reach. In such cases, the product testers are encouraged to publish their assessments in forums, social media, as testimonials or in similar ways.

What is the market like for product testers?

Companies invest a lot of time and money in the development of new products. Ultimately, of course, these investments should pay off as much as possible. In order to guarantee this and, on the other hand, to rule out the possibility of a product flopping, in-depth tests are usually essential before the market launch.

With the help of product tests, companies can check whether their products meet the needs of their customers and fulfill their expectations. Precise pre-publication testing, ideally carried out by people from the target group of the product in question, can reveal any problems with user-friendliness, identify any missing features in terms of functionality, appearance, taste or smell and generally find out what typical buyers really think.

As a result, companies in all sectors are happy to use the services of product testers, which means great potential for them.

How can you earn money with the product tester idea?

Product testers are almost always remunerated for their work. However, this may not be in monetary terms, but with the product itself. After testing, the testers are allowed to keep the product and continue using it. However, the test object is often only provided as a sample or prototype. After the check, such items must be returned to the supplier. In such cases, there is usually an expense allowance.

- Some companies and product tester platforms work with a bonus model: a certain number of points are credited for each review. Once a certain level has been reached, a cash payment can be made.
- Other providers remunerate product testers with a traditional salary or a fixed fee per review.

How much is paid or how many points are awarded depends entirely on the complexity of the test in question. The average payment for beginners is around 25 to 50 francs per check.

What requirements are important for the successful implementation of the product tester idea?

You don't need any training or other special requirements to work as a product tester. However, it is of course important to be able to analyze goods in a meaningful way and to record the relevant findings in a way that is understandable to others. There are often relatively simple questionnaires for such tests. When it comes to making your own opinion public, however, much more know-how is required. In general, a product tester must be able to work precisely according to a briefing.

In principle, it is also an advantage to have your own blog or to be present on the Internet in some other way. Ideally, a product tester should be a self-employed online creator anyway. This makes it easier to work directly with companies and earn money without a special platform as an intermediary. The fee can be significantly higher for this type of cooperation. Well-known influencers can actually earn a lot as product testers. Anyone with this kind of status therefore has a clear advantage.

However, you should have a certain affinity for digital media and content formats, i.e. blogs, social media, photos, videos, etc.. Good (self-)presentation skills are also required. Successful product testers present the tested goods in videos, for example, and must treat them critically (unlike typical influencers, they do not do pure advertising), but still in an all-round respectable way. The line between testers and influencers is de facto thin here.

Photo license seller

Photo license seller as a digital business idea: Provide outstanding images for others and earn money

A photo license seller is first and foremost a photographer or a person who at least has photographic talent. This digital business idea is about taking pictures that can be useful to others and ultimately offering them on the web. Companies - whether they are primarily local businesses or online businesses - always need high-quality photos for their websites. To avoid having to produce these themselves or commission their creation, they like to use images from professional photo license providers.

By purchasing the license for a photograph, the buyer receives certain rights of use. In most cases, they are then free to use the image for their own purposes and sometimes even modify it. As already mentioned, most images are sold online. For beginners, typical image databases or stock photo portals such as Alamy, Shutterstock and iStock Photo are particularly interesting. However, with the right talent, there are also direct cooperation opportunities with companies.

What is the market like for photo license sellers?

"A picture is worth a thousand words": This old metaphor for the added value of images or photos is more relevant today than ever. Especially in the fast-moving Internet, which is now always available thanks to mobile devices, visual content is extremely important. Good images promptly clarify connections, significantly support web designs, can push the usability of online offers and are often the decisive impulse to turn interested parties into buyers.

Licensed images are particularly popular for company websites, as they do not have to be produced in-house and are therefore comparatively inexpensive. Those responsible can choose from a huge catalog in the numerous stock photo portals and are sure to find the right motif. You benefit from high-quality, direct, emotional images that radiate expertise, signal regionality and/or promote usability.

Last but not least, images are extremely relevant to SEO. Google ranks pages that are equipped with contextually appropriate photos better than pages without such content. Good images or other visual components are an indication for the search engine that corresponding offers want to reach their users optimally on several levels. This generally means increased added value for Google.

Since licensed images have a wide range of uses, are practical, can bring many business benefits and ideally even have a beneficial effect on SEO, the sales potential here is quite large. However, it must also be borne in mind that photo license sellers operate in an extremely competitive environment. It is therefore very difficult to earn a living in this area. However, it is relatively easy to earn a certain amount of extra income.

How can you earn money with the photo license seller idea?

In principle, photo license sellers do not offer their images per se, but rather the relevant licenses. This means that several buyers can acquire the rights to use one and the same content. This would not be the case with a direct sale. Licensing is therefore lucrative for providers in the long term. At best, the photos bring in income again and again.

How much you earn depends largely on how you set up your business, the quality of the photos and your experience in the field: if you sell via a stock photo platform, this is very practical for beginners. However, the revenue is rather low due to commission and competition. Direct cooperation with companies or your own store are ideal.

The following three sales channels are particularly common for the online sale of photos.

- **Stock photo portals:** These are platforms on which often thousands of photo license sellers offer their images. Simply register, upload your photos, tag them optimally and wait for buyers.
- **Print services or photo agencies:** Photo license sellers can also make their images available to print services or photo agencies. However,

more experience is often required to have a chance here. Some providers, for example Spreadshirt, make it possible to open a store in the store and then fill it with your own images.

- **Own store:** The direct sale of photos in your own online store can be considered the pinnacle of this business area. Thanks to modular systems, such purchasing channels are fairly easy to create. However, such marketing is usually only worthwhile for professional photographers with a certain reputation.

What requirements are important for a successful implementation of the photo license seller idea?

In the simplest case, i.e. when photos are to be sold via stock portals, it doesn't take much to earn money. A camera, a little talent and registration as a freelancer are enough. You can take photos flexibly, upload them and - if they are of good quality or if the motifs appeal to potential buyers in the best possible way - generate a steady income. However, the earnings here are relatively low.

If you want more, you should be trained as a photographer and offer professional images. If the quality is right and you have a certain amount of experience, you can establish permanent partnerships with photo agencies and consequently receive higher pay. Having your own store can also be worthwhile.

Online Coach

Online coach as a digital business idea: imparting expert knowledge virtually and earning money

A coach is basically an advisor, companion or helping hand in certain matters. As a service provider, their core task is to show their clients the best and most effective ways to achieve their goals. He accompanies the relevant processes from start to finish and uses his input to accelerate the development of those seeking advice. In many cases, the necessary steps can also take place in digital or virtual space.

In such online coaching (or e-coaching), communication between consultants and clients takes place via specific Internet media. There are basically two forms here:

1. Online coaching takes place in addition to face-to-face appointments.

2. Or the consultant uses exclusively digital media for his services.

In the course of e-coaching, various channels can be used for online communication. In most cases, such consultants use video chat software for their work, such as Skype, Facetime or a special coaching platform. However, there are also forms - or often complementary offers - in written form, i.e. by email or messenger, as well as on the phone.

In a live video call, physical and interpersonal aspects - which are very important for many areas of consulting - can be incorporated much more naturally than in telephone coaching, for example, especially body language and the suggestion of a real presence. In order to achieve even better results here, some online coaches use VR glasses and associated software that allow them to "really" face their clients in virtual rooms.

What is the market like for online coaching?

Demand for digital coaching services increased rapidly during the coronavirus pandemic. Previously, such services were still considered a specialty. Of course, it had long been technically possible to receive advice online. However, it was used more as a transitional solution in cases of illness or other problems that prevented coaches and clients from meeting in person. In the meantime, however, communication in virtual space has become an integral part of numerous consulting services. For those interested, this form of coaching is simply particularly convenient. Virtual consultations have become indispensable today.

No wonder, because online coaching has many advantages: As it can take place regardless of location and potentially worldwide, the reach of coaches' services increases enormously. Clients, on the other hand, have the opportunity to access the most value-added coaching services for their needs much more easily. People with certain physical or mobility-related difficulties are generally easier to reach. Coaches and clients save travel time and travel costs. The flexibility of making appointments is significantly greater. Last but not least, short-term or shorter consultations with a higher frequency can be implemented more easily and therefore tend to achieve faster results.

All of this undoubtedly means a lot of potential for online coaching as a digital business idea.

How can you earn money with the online coach idea?

If you want to work as an online coach, you can offer consulting services in numerous areas of life and business. Typical segments are as follows:

- Expansion of leadership skills
- Coaching for self-reflection
- Optimization of the work methodology
- Conversation training and negotiation skills
- Advice on conflict management
- Coaching to increase motivation
- Start-up advice
- Character development
- Burnout prevention

Online coaching is of course not limited to these and similar topics. The following applies: online coaching can be offered with a good chance of success wherever (as many) people as possible have an increased need for support.

What can ultimately be earned depends in particular on the qualifications of the coach and the (financial) relevance of the consulting area. For example, coaching to improve leadership skills is often better paid than support with self-reflection in the private sphere. Career starters can rarely charge more than 50 francs per session. For experienced coaches, however, the fee can easily run into the thousands.

What requirements are important for the successful implementation of the online coach idea?

The professional titles "coach", "consultant" or "trainer" are not protected or do not require training. In contrast to related, more traditional consulting activities, which include working as a lawyer or tax consultant, no officially confirmed qualification is actually required for self-employed work as a coach. Nevertheless, prospective consultants should make sure they have certain professional and personal skills.

In fact, special training or further training as a coach is a decisive sales argument.

For most potential clients, a professional appearance and a professional background are very important. Ideally, you should have references for working as a coach and professional experience in the respective consulting field. In this way, an extremely competent impression and ultimately a high level of trustworthiness can be conveyed in the case of self-employment. The latter is often decisive in coaching. If those seeking advice do not feel that they are in good hands, they will hardly recognize any potential for achieving personal or professional benefits with the consultant in question. Basically, the better coaching service providers present themselves, the greater the chances of attracting many clients and the higher the fee can be set.

Online video courses

Online video courses as a digital business idea: offer training on demand and earn money

Online video courses or training sessions are usually spread over several sessions and therefore often spread over several days or even weeks. The main aim of such service providers is to provide participants or clients with targeted knowledge or skills on the topic in question using various methods.

The course provider does not have to communicate live with the participants. It is also possible to offer courses in real time and at fixed times (whereby the boundaries to online coaching are often blurred). However, online video courses are often recorded and then made available to interested parties for flexible access. The orientation is generally more in the format of a lecture and less as a seminar with direct exchange. Nevertheless, modern online training courses often give participants the opportunity to write comments or ask direct questions.

In general, today's online video courses use a variety of media to be entertaining and interesting for their target groups and ultimately achieve the best results for them. Video recordings form the basis. However, texts or handouts, whitepapers etc., audio files or interactive programs, e-mail, telephone, live chats and even VR are also sometimes integrated.

What is the market like for online video courses?

Courses and further education, training and courses no longer take place exclusively in the form of face-to-face events. In fact, many interested parties now prefer digital offerings. Online video courses have been on the rise since the coronavirus pandemic, when educational and training institutions or private training service providers were no longer allowed to hold events on site. E-learning, and therefore self-directed learning, has become so established over this period that it is now standard in many areas.

Online video courses are particularly practical. Above all, they can be used at any time and from anywhere. Participants benefit from independence of location, which means great flexibility in terms of time. There are no travel costs for the participants and fewer expenses for rooms for the organizers. This makes such offers generally relatively inexpensive. As the sessions are usually recorded, clients do not have to wonder whether their course is actually taking place. Once the course is online, they can access it at any time and learn at their own pace. This supports motivation and effectiveness. If something is not clear the first time, it is no problem to simply repeat the session.

All in all, online video courses offer a great deal of learning convenience and even tend to lead to particularly useful results. It is therefore not surprising that more and more potential clients expect further training courses to have a digital focus and now even prefer to use them. This means a lot of sales opportunities for the relevant service providers.

How can you earn money with the online video course idea?

Online video courses can be offered on a wide range of topics. The basic prerequisite is that there is an increased interest in the focused direction and that people are willing to spend money on the program. The chances of earning money are generally quite good, as there is actually an increased interest in appropriate assistance today (partly due to the increasingly complex everyday and professional lives of many people).

Popular areas are the following:

- Business and leadership
- Health and medicine
- Alternative medicine
- Spirituality
- Hobby and exercise
- Fashion and lifestyle
- Psychology and coping with life
- Animals and animal health

There are many examples in German-speaking countries that show that online video courses not only generate additional income, but can even be used to earn a living. Certain educational offers in the fields of "health", "business" or "veterinary medicine" have been proven to generate annual sales of up to 100,000 euros. Such successes are of course not the rule, but with a good idea and strategy, a lot can be achieved financially.

Beginners should not sell themselves short. If there is interest and reach, 100 francs or more per participant can be charged, depending on the relevance of the topic, the expertise imparted and the scope of the course. For experienced providers of online video courses with a good reputation, the sky is the limit.

What requirements are important for the successful implementation of the online video course idea?

A successful online video course offering must fulfill very similar conditions to online coaching. The keys to many paying customers are a perfectly developed topic with the highest possible relevance and the creation of trust. The latter is primarily conveyed through genuine expertise in the relevant field. The completion of special training and/or professional experience in the respective segment are decisive factors here.

Many newcomers find it particularly difficult to find the right topic. Ideally, personal skills and interests should first be scrutinized when deciding on a topic. Ultimately, trust and credibility once again play a central role.

Can you demonstrate real expertise in a field? Do you have know-how in a subject area that interests many people? Do you have a passion for a particular topic? If you start by answering these questions and find a suitable direction, you will not only provide a corresponding course offering with optimum added value, but also run it with great enthusiasm. This enthusiasm is automatically passed on to customers.

This is important both financially and in terms of work motivation. You should bear in mind that you will probably be dealing with one topic for a long time and that it is of little use to look for an area in which there is a lot of money to be made, but which you yourself hardly find interesting. After all, customers would also notice and negatively perceive such a misalignment.

Webinars

Webinars as a digital business idea: offer seminars online and earn money

The word "webinar" describes almost perfectly what this education method is all about: it is a seminar that takes place on the web. Such training courses are held on specific overarching topics and are usually organized by one person as a moderator or seminar leader. These responsible persons share their knowledge and skills in the respective focused area with the participants. In this respect, webinars are similar to online video courses or digital consulting services. However, in contrast to video training courses, they are usually held live and, unlike coaching sessions, have a more educational and less advisory character.

Specific webinar software is often used for the implementation. This enables the flexible scaling of participant numbers as well as the organization of registrations and provides many functions that help to design, make more interesting and promote corresponding offers. At such events, it is fundamentally important that participants can also interact with each other. This also distinguishes the webinar from the video course, where communication with the provider is normally comparatively limited.

An optimal webinar is similar to an on-site training event. It offers an optimal audiovisual environment, features to illustrate content and the opportunity for uncomplicated interaction.

What is the market like for webinars?

In principle, webinars have a similar market relevance to other online education and consulting services, especially video courses and coaching. At the latest after the coronavirus restrictions, more and more people no longer want to do without such options. Digital options are even preferred for certain groups and individual areas.

In the context of webinars, this is primarily due to the special advantages they have over on-site seminars. The areas of application or topics of such courses are practically unlimited. Almost anything can be taught over the Internet with the help of suitable technical aids: from hobby or leisure courses in the areas of technology, sport, interior design and nutrition to university seminars and training courses or further training in technical professions.

The participants are not tied to a specific location, but can still be shown facts, interact and even watch certain content again and again in a recording for better understanding.

Under these conditions, the chances of being successful with a perfectly developed webinar idea are more than good.

How can you earn money with the webinar idea?

In order to monetize webinars, they are usually offered for a fee. In order to achieve good sales opportunities despite the large number of free offers in many subject areas today, it is important to convey outstanding added value and a great deal of trust.

In the best-case scenario, organizers can charge hundreds or even thousands of euros per participant. However, it takes quite a while to get that far. The more experience and expertise there is in the area being taught and the more relevant the subject matter (personal, professional, social, etc.), the greater the income will generally be.

Webinars are generally booked in connection with the transfer of knowledge in complex or even scientific matters. However, there is also considerable demand in everyday matters.

Typical domains for webinars are as follows:

- Company foundation
- Online marketing
- Personal development
- Design and architecture

- Presenting and speaking in front of people
- Career or business growth
- Technology and innovation
- Fashion and lifestyle
- Handicraft and art
- Nutrition and health
- Photography and film
- Love and relationships
- Personal income and finances
- Alternative medicine, yoga or meditation

What requirements are important for the successful implementation of the webinar idea?

As with the delivery of online video courses and digital coaching, finding the perfect topic and instilling confidence are extremely important key elements for the financially successful delivery of webinars.

Such training courses should also be particularly well designed. The appearance of a webinar proves to be almost as crucial as the information that is conveyed. Today's society is generally very visually oriented, which means that images, graphics, overall branding, etc. often make the difference, even for online services (of all kinds). This applies not only during the sessions, but also when promoting them. Within webinars, it is indeed extremely important to use many visual and, at best, intuitively understandable elements. This makes the often complex topics much more accessible and attractive.

The perfect presentation and effective teaching in general require specific didactic and design skills.

Interested parties should therefore invest in a professional webinar platform that enables them to integrate impressive visual motifs and also consider training their skills as teachers themselves.

E-BOOKS

E-books as a digital business idea: earning money with electronic non-fiction, fiction and more

An e-book is a book in electronic form that can be consumed via special readers or other digital devices such as smartphones, tablets and desktop computers. Such works are available either as an alternative to a hardback edition or as a stand-alone edition. Those who want to earn money with e-books as a digital business idea usually focus on the latter option.

The great advantage here lies in the fact that such books are particularly quick and easy to produce and distribute. It doesn't take much more than a text program and Internet access to put ideas on paper and find a suitable publisher or distribution channel.

Professional e-books are typographically set and designed in the same way as printed books, which means that the amount of work involved is correspondingly greater. It is also possible to introduce complex forms of presentation or multimedia content that lead to exceptional reading experiences. However, this is by no means necessary for the beginning and the first earnings.

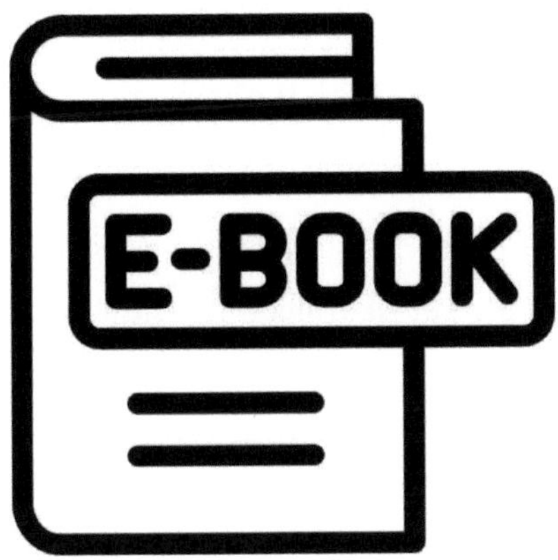

What is the market like for e-books?

The demand for e-books is indeed enormous: market analyses speak of a volume of more than 16 billion US dollars. The 20 billion mark is expected to be significantly exceeded by 2028.

The global e-book market is being driven primarily by the ever-improving reading devices, which have long offered a similar experience to real books, and technical innovations for new display elements. In addition, people have less and less time to go to a bookstore, and the quick download of a digital work is simply unbeatably convenient.

- Readers can access millions of books from every conceivable genre via special e-book libraries or similar online services. This is not only a convenient, but also a cost-effective alternative to traditional purchasing or delivery methods. The prices are more than reasonable via electronic lending.

- Once again, the pandemic has - or rather had - a major impact on sales of electronic books. During the lockdown, many people returned to old entertainment values that they found in e-books, even without having to enter a store. E-book sales soared - and many readers simply stuck with the convenience of digital books after the restrictions.

All of this makes it clear what huge potential there is in the e-book idea.

How can you earn money with the e-book idea?

Of course, e-books first have to be written, which is the most time-consuming part of the idea. Once this work is done, the works can be distributed relatively easily via Amazon or other online retailers. Not much more than a registration is required here.

Alternatively, it is of course also possible to organize sales via your own websites (including social media). This gives authors the opportunity to offer their books free of charge, but to generate income through advertising or affiliate links. Ideally, the companies or products in question should be in the same subject area as the e-book in question.

Logically, how much you can ultimately earn with a digital book depends heavily on price and demand. A clever calculation is extremely important here: for example, if an e-book costs CHF 10 and is sold 100 times, that's CHF 1,000 in earnings (minus retailer commission and taxes). In terms of the work put into the book, that's not very much.

Experienced e-book authors therefore often rely on less extensive books or e-papers in parallel. There is a more than decent market here, as many people are not prepared (or have the time) to read an entire book in every information or entertainment context.

What requirements are important for the successful implementation of the e-book idea?

Writing and publishing an e-book requires a lot of time (in addition to a distribution channel and a clever cost calculation) and, last but not least, a good strategy. The latter is important in order to be able to write productively even with many deadlines in everyday life.

Ideally, you should create a fixed amount of free time for copywriting each day or week (depending on how quickly you want the results). Once these working hours have been defined, it is important to find the right flow. Of course, the starting point should above all be a topic that ideally meets with increased interest from a larger target group. Beginners in particular are then well advised to start by writing individual articles or chapters that will ultimately be compiled into an e-book.

Although this is not particularly creative, it is extremely effective. This results in certain milestones and real conclusions that motivate you to continue. In addition, the sections are likely to generate additional ideas that constantly expand the added value of the book, allowing the work to grow automatically and enabling readers to benefit even more from a purchase. Even the great writer Mark Twain is said to have been successful with this technique in his day.

E-SPORTS

E-sports as a digital business idea: earn money as a professional by participating in video game tournaments

The term "e-sports" stands for "electronic sports", although these are not necessarily specific or real sports that take place electronically or digitally, but rather matches or championships in which players and teams face each other in very different video games.

So it doesn't necessarily have to be a football or basketball video game. Shooters or strategy games can also be played as part of e-sports. The word "sport" is used here to describe the competitive or tournament nature of the events.

Just as is the case with professionals in real sports, e-athletes can also be paid for their performances in major competitions. And just as with real athletes, fees and prize money increase the better the players are in their field. In fact, the cracks in the scene can not only make a very good living from their profession, they are even multi-millionaires.

What is the market like for e-sports?

The e-sports market has been on the upswing for years: revenues in the areas of merchandising, ticket sales, sponsorship, media rights, advertising, game publisher fees and others will amount to a whopping 1.7 billion US dollars in 2023: This is suggested by various statistics. This does not include the prize money brokered for players and teams. These are in a league of their own. At The International alone, the largest Dota tournament in the world, prize pools of more than 40 million US dollars have been achieved in the past.

There are many reasons for this boom: matches are increasingly being streamed or broadcast on TV. There is remarkable investment on the part of organizers, promoters and teams. League tournament infrastructures are being increasingly perfected and viewer numbers are rising immensely, both on site and during broadcasts. On Twitch alone, the largest live streaming platform for gamers, fans now watch more than 20 billion hours of e-sports per year. Sales are also growing, especially with the increasing interest. Colleges and universities have even started to offer specific programs to develop and promote qualified professionals in the e-sports sector.

All of this means enormous potential for e-sports professionals. In particular, the huge prize pools of international tournaments make professional participation in electronic sports a very common career aspiration.

How can you earn money with the e-sports idea?

The major difficulty in terms of payment for e-sports activities is finding a team or sponsor that will ultimately enable a regular salary to be collected.

Budding professionals are initially left to their own devices. They often start their career in individual games on the Internet. They should climb the rankings confidently and high up the ladder and impress at amateur tournaments. If you perform well, there is a real chance that team managers or scouts will take notice and invitations to trial training sessions or larger castings will arrive.

This is where you have to prove your skills under increased pressure. Professional teams take great care to ensure that their members remain calm even under particular stress and still make full use of their skills. The best social skills are also a key point for those responsible. E-sports has a lot to do with cooperation, cohesion and communication. Dealing with fellow players should be impeccable.

Those who perform optimally in all areas and meet the requirements of the team leaders are ultimately accepted as members and receive a monthly salary. Successful professionals earn additional money through the often enormous tournament prize money. They are also celebrated stars in the scene, which can bring individual sponsorship contracts, engagements as advertising ambassadors and generally ideal conditions for income as influencers.

What requirements are important for the successful implementation of the e-sports idea?

In order to become a professional e-sportsman and be successful in the long term, interested parties must have many of the same qualities as professionals in conventional sports. Naturally, there should be a great affinity for popular e-sports games. Specialization is an important prerequisite for big earnings and prize money. Furthermore, e-sports cracks are extremely ambitious, disciplined, focused and, last but not least, very good team players with strong communication skills.

After all, their main activity is not simply playing games on a console or PC for fun. Like professional basketball players, golfers, tennis players or footballers, they focus entirely on their sport. They are experts in certain multiplayer titles from specific tournament genres, such as real-time strategy or sports simulation. Getting to a competitive level here means real work.

Such professionals play for many hours every day and become intensively familiar with all game elements. The relevant movement sequences and control commands are literally internalized and become automatic and reflexive. Depending on the game, daily training in front of the screen often consists of sequences for honing reaction skills, proactive speed of action and/or aiming accuracy.

It is also important to study the behavior of other players and draw conclusions for your own gameplay or team. In this way, ideas, tactics and strategies, which of course also need to be pursued, are constantly being perfected. Everything to surprise the opponent and ultimately defeat them with confidence.

Online Marketer

Online marketer as a digital business idea: offer online marketing expertise or use it yourself to earn money

Online marketers are experts in online marketing. As a rule, they are familiar with several disciplines in the field and offer their know-how as a service provider or use it (in parallel) for their own purposes.

The central topics and areas of work that fall within the online marketer's field of activity are SEO, SEA, social media advertising, usability and conversion optimization, content marketing, video marketing, e-mail marketing, affiliate marketing, mobile marketing, customer relationship marketing, corporate identity, corporate design and social media marketing.

In fact, hardly any self-employed professional covers all of these domains completely. For professional success, however, you should have a good knowledge of at least most areas.

What is the market like for online marketers?

In all kinds of areas of life, people are increasingly using digital helpers and the internet to make everyday tasks easier, fulfill wishes or overcome problems. For most people, search engines are now the primary point of contact for obtaining information in a wide variety of contexts. Apps help with cooking, sports or shopping. And even communication habits are increasingly shifting towards digital messengers or social networks.

For the companies in the background, all of this is largely about one thing: selling. Search engines offer advertising space, online stores want to sell as many of their products as possible to the respective target group, app or software providers aim to use premium licenses and there is also a lot of money in social media with influencers, social selling and the like. The list could go on almost indefinitely.

In order to benefit optimally from this enormous market potential, the (digital) goods or services sold must be publicized on a broad front, presented in a positive light and all technical requirements, effects and interactions must be perfectly harmonized. This is exactly where online marketers come into play. They hold the reins as managers and/or carry out central tasks themselves.

In Switzerland, too, the corresponding demand is growing continuously as online activities continue to expand in all areas of business. The turnover to be generated with digital advertising alone is estimated at around CHF 3.2 billion by 2027. This not only means enormous potential for the companies concerned, but also for independent online marketers.

The latter also benefit considerably from the fact that not every company can or wants to hire a professional for such marketing tasks, and yet all those who want to be competitive on the market in the long term must invest in digital customer acquisition and retention.

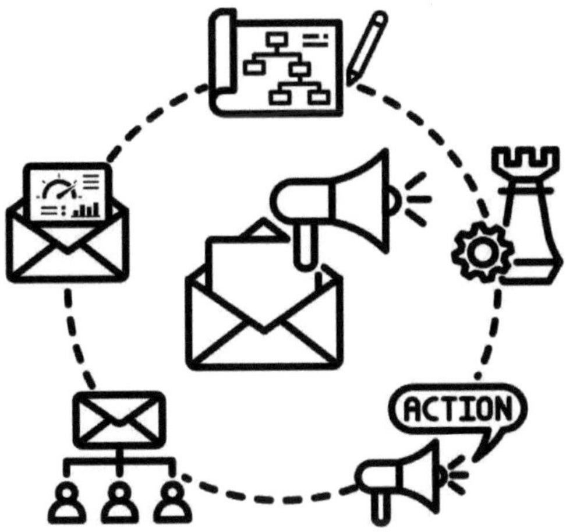

How can you earn money with the online marketer idea?

There are various ways to earn an income as an online marketer.

The great advantage that self-employed people have is that they are not restricted to earning money in just one way. They can and should combine several options to ensure a secure turnover.

The following professional orientations are typical:

1. **Online marketers as service providers:** As freelancers, online marketers can work with companies and support them in various areas of online marketing. This can include, for example, the management of social media channels, search engine optimization for Google and/or the creation of blog texts.
2. **Coaching and consulting:** Coaches and consultants pass on their

know-how and experience to marketing managers in companies or other interested parties. The aim is usually to get customers to implement their online marketing work in-house in the medium to long term.

3. **Affiliate marketing:** To be able to run successful affiliate marketing independently, a broad knowledge of online marketing is essential. Affiliate marketers basically perform many tasks that are also the responsibility of online marketers as freelancers. They promote third-party goods or services on their own websites. In return, they receive a commission every time a contract is concluded.

What requirements are important for the successful implementation of the online marketer idea?

To be successful as an online marketer, you need to have certain skills. Ideally, of course, you should have a university education and some practical experience in the field. The latter factor is usually more decisive than the former.

Professionals who have a proven track record as employees in online marketing are of course particularly popular as freelancers. On the other hand, they can also implement their own projects, for example in affiliate marketing, more efficiently and ultimately more quickly and profitably. Otherwise, a good reputation in customer reviews, project references and an optimal (self-initiated) online presence is very helpful. Beginners in particular should pay more attention to gaining such "capital".

In principle, however, the job title "online marketer" is not tied to a specific education or other qualifications. Anyone who knows how to optimize a website for Google, what it takes to achieve business success in social networks and/or how to create advantageous content for online presences can call themselves an online marketer. In general, however, this profession requires a broader knowledge of online marketing, i.e. across several disciplines. For example, if the expertise is more in the area of search engine optimization, it is a good idea to narrow it down to "SEO expert" in order to tell potential customers directly what they can and cannot expect. The same applies to other specializations.

WEB & APP PROGRAMMING

Web and app programming as a digital business idea: create online applications and generate income

Web and app programming deals with the creation of high-quality or value-added digital applications. The latter usually relate to the solution of problems or wishes of consumers or companies. Professional programmers - also known as developers - take care of the development, maintenance and further training of corresponding applications. As freelancers, they usually work closely with companies that require a web application or app, or with agencies that sell the relevant services and products.

Developers are proficient in common web, scripting and programming languages such as HTML5, CSS, JavaScript, PHP, Python, Ruby, etc. In addition, web and app programmers have a good understanding of media-specific usability and user experience factors. They write code, advise customers, develop the possibilities of existing applications and work on strategies - depending on their training, specialist knowledge and level of experience.

What is the market like for web and app programmers?

Digital media - and in particular online applications such as web applications or mobile apps - are on the rise in all areas of daily life. This applies to both the private and business/professional environment. Accordingly, there is a great need for specialists to create, develop and maintain such systems.

In fact, there is a real shortage of developers. The Job Market Monitor Switzerland from the University of Zurich *ranks developers and analysts of software and IT applications among the most sought-after occupational groups in 2023. Alongside specialists in the healthcare professions, this is where the "most acute shortage of skilled workers" exists.*

The huge demand, combined with the clear deficit, naturally offers free-lancers excellent prospects for a stable order situation.

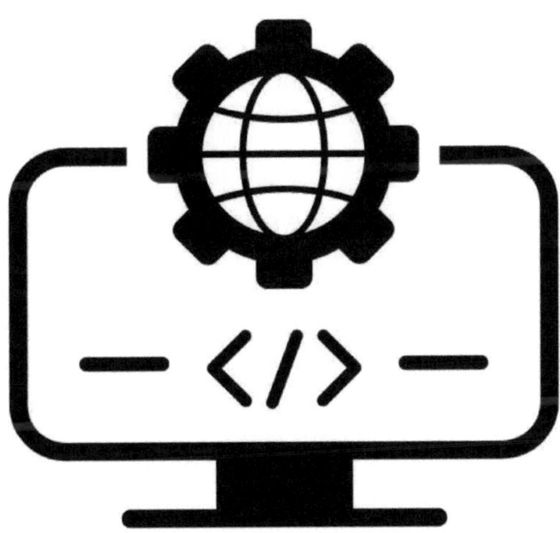

How can you earn money with the web and app programmer idea?

A freelance web and app programmer is responsible for getting enough jobs and earning enough money to make a living. This is not an easy task, but it also offers a lot of freedom and a great deal of work flexibility.

There are basically two ways to earn a regular income as a developer:

1. **Companies or agencies offer developer services:** Typically, web and app programmers work with companies that require a corresponding application or with agencies from the service sector. It is particularly useful for newcomers to use freelancer networks to find suitable projects, customers and partners. Smaller companies in particular often search for suitable specialists on such portals. It is generally not profitable for them to employ developers on a permanent basis. In some cases, however, there are also large corporations that would like to benefit from fresh ideas and unconventional approaches from an outsider. In principle, there are two different processes. In most cases, freelancers apply for specific projects that are advertised on the relevant portals. However, companies or agencies also approach experienced developers with a good reputation themselves.

2. **Develop and market your own projects or products:** There are thousands of web or app solutions for a wide variety of needs. Before their release, hardly anyone would have guessed how popular they would ultimately become. Developing and distributing such a hit and perennial favorite is the dream of many developers. If you have sufficient market intuition, creativity and talent, you can certainly work towards initiating your own projects that either break new ground or address familiar demands. However, this option is of course quite risky. This is because you are working into the blue, so to speak - without a contract or a specific requirement profile. This is why very few professionals focus entirely on their own projects. They tend to be used as an additional way of securing contract work.

What requirements are important for the successful implementation of the web and app programmer idea?

The classic career of a web and app programmer begins either with an apprenticeship, for example as a computer scientist for application development, or by studying at a university. In addition to general academic computer science, there are now special, practical courses such as coding and software engineering.

One of the great advantages of working as a freelance developer is that a completed education and a strong CV are not mandatory requirements. Programmers are often career changers without a traditional IT education. Even autodidacts can have a good chance of getting developer jobs. There are many distance learning courses or further education courses that increase potential.

Nevertheless, certain professional experience and/or (project) references or positive reviews from customers and partners are of course very important for successful self-employment. If you really want to be booked frequently, you have to prove yourself first. Beginners in particular should therefore work hard to build up as good a reputation as possible that is visible to the public.

ONLY FANS

Only fans as a digital business idea: earning money through subscriptions as a content creator

Only Fans is a special social network and a popular platform for content creators. The service is primarily used for the distribution of erotic content, but there are certainly alternative application contexts. As in many other social media channels, photos or videos or impressions from the lives and work of participants are often posted, liked and commented on.

However, the focus here is clearly on "creating" in the sense of work and the clear goal of generating income with corresponding goods. Facebook, X (formerly Twitter) and Instagram are primarily designed for private interactions and only offer various additional options for monetization. In contrast, earning money is quite clearly the main focus with Only Fans. Most people who use the service to display their content do so for a fee. They sell images, video clips, audio content, but also information or specialist knowledge and other resources to be provided digitally.

To this end, Only Fans offers a specific subscription system through which profiles can be made accessible for a fee: This means that fans have to pay a certain monthly fee to be able to view the content.

What is the market like for Only Fans?

Only Fans has recorded steadily increasing user numbers since its launch in 2016. Since 2018, the company's focus has been primarily on explicit adult content, once again confirming an old advertising adage: Sex sells!

In 2019, the platform had around 13.5 million users. Today, in 2023, there are a whopping 323.5 million, which represents an increase of more than 2,000% in four years - and the trend is still rising. The entire user base now spends an average of almost five billion dollars a year on the service (reference year 2022). This makes it one of the most financially successful tech start-ups in recent years.

This naturally means enormous potential for active content providers. The latter is evidenced not least by the frequent reports of very generous revenues for certain participants. Popular content frequently generates income of several thousand or even tens of thousands of dollars per month.

How can you earn money with the Only Fans idea?

With Only Fans, payment is made via a specific subscription system. The providers themselves decide how much access to their content costs per month. Of the final earnings, 20 percent goes to the company and 80 percent to the content creators. The more fans or followers there are, the greater the income. In addition to the sale of subscriptions, income can be generated through tips or the offer of private communication. It is also possible to provide completely individualized products to very interested parties.

The most successful content on Only Fans is - and will probably remain - erotic in nature. It doesn't always have to be "naked". However, those who have a certain attractiveness and charisma and can showcase both well generally have the best chances of making good money.

It is true that the recurring revenue records are often set by Only Fans participants whose content is at least not directly related to the explicit erotic genre. However, the people in question are usually stars or starlets with an international reputation. These include, for example, the US actress and singer Bella Thorne, who, according to her own information, raised two million dollars via the platform within a week after going online with Only Fans in August 2020. Success stories like this are the absolute exception, but are naturally very attractive to most interested parties.

In keeping with the "physical" focus of the network, many successful influencers from the sports, fitness or modeling sector use Only Fans as an additional channel to generate additional income from particularly loyal followers. The concept behind this is as simple as it is ingenious: the user is given more exclusive insights and closer contact with the person offering them. Real fans are only too happy to take advantage of these opportunities.

All in all, the range of professions, hobbies and other activities with which you can earn money on Only Fans is very broad: Musicians, dancers, chefs, fitness trainers, personal coaches, technology experts and many others offer their products via the platform. The products are not always just photos or videos of the people themselves. Cooking courses are given, workouts are arranged, individual consultations are provided and, and, and. Finally, there are even crowdfunding initiatives and appeals for donations.

What requirements are important for the successful implementation of the Only Fans idea?

In order to generate reliable income with Only Fans, it is advisable to create and follow a long-term social media strategy on which all activities are based. The following points are fundamental:

- Creating an appealing profile and updating it regularly.
- Continuous publication of new content (preferably daily) that justifies the subscription costs.
- Precisely serving the expectations of your own fans in content paired with new ideas and unique characteristics.
- The use of other social networks for promotional purposes with teasers for content on Only Fans.

Glossary

A

- **Affiliate marketing:** Performance-based marketing in which commissions are paid for referred sales or leads.
- **A/B testing:** Comparison of two variants (A and B) of a website, landing page or email to determine the better performance.
- **AdSense:** Google's advertising program that enables website operators to sell advertising space on their website.
- **Ads:** Google's online advertising platform that allows companies to place ads in Google search results and on other websites.
- **App Store Optimization (ASO):** Optimization of apps for search in the app stores to increase visibility and download figures.

B

- **Backlink:** Link from one website to another website. Backlinks are an important factor for search engine optimization (SEO).
- **Behavioral targeting:** Alignment of advertising to the usage behavior of users, e.g. websites visited or search terms.
- **Big data:** Collecting and analyzing large volumes of data to gain insights for marketing.

- **Blog:** Online diary or journal in which new posts are published regularly.
- **Bounce rate:** The rate of visitors who leave a website after just one visit.
- **Brand marketing:** Marketing with the aim of improving brand awareness and brand image.

C

- **Call to action (CTA):** Request to the user to perform a specific action, e.g. to click a button or fill out a form.
- **Content marketing:** Creation and distribution of valuable content to attract and retain customers.
- **Conversion rate:** The rate of visitors who perform a desired action, e.g. complete a purchase or submit a form.
- **Cookie:** Small text file that is stored on the user's computer to collect information about their usage behavior.
- **Cost per click (CPC):** Payment model for online advertising in which the advertiser pays a certain amount per click on their ad.
- **Cost per lead (CPL):** Payment model for online advertising in which the advertiser pays a certain amount per lead generated.
- **Cost per mille (CPM):** Payment model for online advertising in which the advertiser pays a certain amount per 1,000 impressions of their ad.
- **Customer Acquisition Cost (CAC):** The cost of acquiring a new customer.
- **Customer Lifetime Value (CLV):** The total revenue generated by a customer during their entire business relationship with a company.

D

- **Data-driven marketing:** Marketing that makes decisions based on data analysis.

- **Demand generation:** Generating interest and demand for a product or service.
- **Digital analytics:** Analysis of customers' online behavior in order to gain insights for marketing.
- **Digital business model:** Business model based on the use of digital technologies.
- **Direct marketing:** Addressing customers directly by e-mail, telephone or post.
- **Display advertising:** Advertising in the form of banners, videos or other visual elements.
- **Domain:** Name of a website, e.g. www.google.com: https://www.go ogle.com.

E

- **E-commerce:** online trade in goods and services.
- **E-mail marketing:** Sending e-mails to customers and interested parties to inform them about products, offers or news.

F

- **Facebook Ads:** Facebook's advertising platform that allows companies to place ads on Facebook and Instagram.
- **Google Analytics:** Tool for analyzing website traffic.
- **Google Search Console:** Tool for optimizing the website for search engines.
- **Guerrilla marketing:** unconventional and cost-effective marketing methods.

I

- **Inbound marketing:** Marketing strategy aimed at attracting and retaining customers through valuable content.

- **Influencer marketing:** Collaboration with influencers to promote products or services.
- **Instagram Ads:** Instagram's advertising platform that allows companies to place ads on Instagram.

K

- Conversion: Completion of a desired action by the user, e.g. completing a purchase or submitting a form.

L

- Landing page: Website page that users are taken to after clicking on an ad or link.
- Lead: Contact information of a potential customer.
- Long-tail keywords: Keywords with a low search volume but high relevance.

M

- Marketing automation: Automation of marketing processes, e.g . email marketing or lead generation.
- Mobile marketing: Marketing on mobile devices such as smartphones and tablets.

N

- Native advertising: Advertising that adapts to the environment in which it appears.
- Network effect: Phenomenon in which the value of a product or service increases with the number of users.
- Niche marketing: Focusing on a specific target group with special needs.

O

- Offline marketing: Marketing activities that are not carried out via the Internet.

- Online marketing: All marketing activities that are carried out via the Internet.
- Opt-in: Consent of the user to receive emails from a company.

P

- Pay-per-click (PPC): Payment model for online advertising in which the advertiser pays a certain amount per click on their ad.
- Personal branding: Building a personal brand to position yourself as an expert in a particular field.
- Product marketing: Marketing for a specific product or service.
- Public Relations (PR): Building and maintaining relationships with the media and the public.

R

- Referral marketing: Marketing strategy in which customers are rewarded for recommending a product or service.
- Remarketing: Addressing users who have already interacted with a company.
- Retargeting: Addressing users who have visited a website or app with advertising on other websites or apps.
- Return on investment (ROI): Key figure for measuring the success of a marketing measure.

S

- Search Engine Marketing (SEM): Marketing in search engines such as Google and Bing.
- Search Engine Optimization (SEO): Optimization of a website for search engines to improve visibility in search results.
- Social media marketing: Use of social media platforms such as

Facebook, Twitter and Instagram for marketing purposes.

- Social selling: Use of social media platforms for the direct sale of products or services.
- Storytelling: Using stories to build an emotional bond with customers.

T

- Testimonial: Customer review or statement used to increase the credibility of a product or service.
- Thought leadership: Positioning as an expert in a particular field to build trust and authority.
- Traffic: Number of visitors to a website.
- Tracking: Recording of user behavior on a website, e.g. pages visited and links clicked on.

U

- Usability: user-friendliness of a website or app.

V

- Viral marketing: Marketing strategy that aims to get content shared and distributed by users.

W

- Website: Collection of linked web pages that can be accessed under one domain.

Z

- Target group: Group of people who are to be addressed with a marketing measure.